A Western Horseman Book
Colorado Springs, Colorado

CUTTING

By Leon Harrel

with Randy Witte

Photographs by Darrell Arnold

CUTTING

Published by
The Western Horseman, Inc.

3850 North Nevada Avenue
P.O. Box 7980
Colorado Springs, CO 80933-7980

Design, Typography, and Production
Western Horseman
Colorado Springs, Colorado

Printing
Williams Printing
Colorado Springs, Colorado

ISBN 0-911647-15-5

DEDICATION

I dedicate this book to my loving wife, Myrna, and my children, Hollie, Lesa, LaDonna, and Lance, for their love and trust in me. They have been my inspiration in life. At a time when I wanted to quit, they gave their love and faith, giving me the confidence to accomplish anything and everything in life I wanted. I thank God for being my silent partner in life, guiding me through my successes and failures.

ACKNOWLEDGEMENTS

There are three men I would like to acknowledge.
One is a man by the name of Robert L. Waltrip, for stepping forward, offering me his support and friendship, having faith in me at the darkest point of my career.
The second is Jack Hightower, for giving me his friendship and support every time I have asked for it or every time I have needed it.
The last, but by no means the least, is my good friend Larry Mahan, who is a living legend of proof that champions are forever.

Leon Harrel
LEON HARREL

On the cover: an action photo of Leon Harrel and the winning mare, Smart Date.

CONTENTS

Page 6   **1/INTRODUCTION**

Page 12   **2/HOW TO GET STARTED**

Page 16   **3/EQUIPMENT**

Page 20   **4/HOW TO RIDE**

Page 30   **5/JUDGING AND SCORING**

Page 36   **6/CATTLE**

Page 40   7/Showing and Winning

Page 48   8/Training

Page 130   9/Great Horses

Page 132   10/Profile: Leon Harrel

Page 142   11/Terminology

1 INTRODUCTION

Leon Harrel, a man who has literally "done it all" in cutting, is a strong proponent of this family sport, and an excellent teacher.

What It's All About

Leon Harrel sat relaxed in the saddle atop a young mare named Smart Date as spectators poured into Will Rogers Coliseum in Fort Worth. The audience was there to watch the finals of the open division of the 1987 National Cutting Horse Association Futurity. Leon and Smart Date were among the 23 finalists out of 375 entries.

A bystander walked up to Leon and shook his hand. "Been hearing some good things about the way this mare is working, " he said.

"I think she'll do it," Leon smiled. "We'll find out tonight."

Leon walked the mare back inside the warmup ring at one end of the arena. A herd of cattle was being settled at the other end, and the cutting would begin in about 30 minutes. The cattle, all yearling heifers, were chosen for their uniformity in weight and size. The first 11 cutters would work this herd, then a fresh bunch of cattle would be brought in for the remaining 12 cutters. Five judges, secluded from each other and from the scoreboard, would score each cutter from 60 to 80 points; the highest and lowest scores would be thrown out, and the middle three scores added. As in all cutting competitions, the best-scoring cutter would win first place.

The contest has total prize money each year that approaches $2 million. The top pro cutters in the world are entered, along with hundreds of non-professionals who compete in separate divisions. A non-pro is classified as such if he doesn't train cutting horses for remuneration of any kind. But the real stars of the two-week competition are the horses, all three-year-olds who are there to show their inherent cow sense and what they've learned after a little more than a year of training. When horse and rider enter the herd to separate one cow from the others, and the rider drops his rein hand to the horse's neck, what happens next is largely up to the cow and the horse.

People get hooked on riding cutting horses, and watching them work, when they discover that cutting is exhilarating and fun to do. Beyond that, it is an equine sport with roots as a ranch chore—sorting cattle in the open for various reasons—and it has been likened to an art form. The horse becomes a willing, thinking athlete, in partnership with the horseman, who is simply along for the ride. At its best, the partnership works like this: The horse cuts whatever cow the rider selects, and then prevents the cow from getting back to the herd by mirroring its moves, left and right—by running, stopping, reversing directions—all on a loose rein. Ideally, the horse will completely control the cow in the center of the arena. In return for all the horse does, the rider basically has to maintain a good seat in the saddle, and stay out of the horse's way, not hinder his movements.

As a team, horse and rider have 2½ minutes to work in front of a judge, or judges, and they'll typically cut and work one cow, then go back into the herd to cut a second cow, and sometimes a third cow. A cutter is penalized for mistakes, like letting a cow that's being worked slip by and get back to the herd, or for visibly cueing the horse, like raising the rein hand while a cow is being worked.

The cutter has four helpers, all horseback, while he is working in the arena. A herd holder is stationed on each side of the herd to prevent the cattle from moving up the fence. And two turnback riders are positioned farther out in the arena to encourage the cow that is being worked to not simply run off to the far end. At any contest, whether the cattle are fresh (have never before been used in cutting) or not, the cutter wants to try to select a cow (or calf—the terminology is

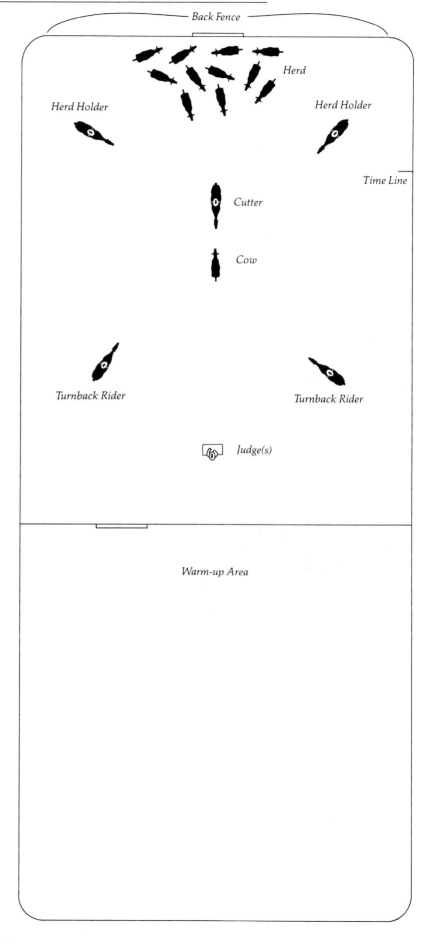

Leon and Smart Date, winning the 1987 NCHA Futurity.   **NCHA Photo by Pat Hall**

interchangeable, but the animals are typically yearling or two-year-old steers or heifers) that hasn't been cut by another contestant. The more that cattle are cut, the more they tend to simply run while being worked, or just give up and not move, rather than test the horse in the middle of the arena, where the best scores are earned.

At the Futurity finals, Leon Harrel and Smart Date had drawn up to cut last in the first section. That meant ten other cutters would go before them. One of Leon's herd holders had placed himself where he could watch the cattle, and when Leon rode into the herd for his first cut, clock running, the man pointed out a cow that hadn't been worked. Leon took his time, going deep into the herd and bringing the cow out with a bunch of others; slowly the cattle flowed back around on both sides, returning to the others, and Leon maneuvered carefully and quietly until the last calf in front of him was the one he wanted. Then he lowered his rein hand, and Smart Date dropped her head and went to work.

The performance on that cow lasted well over 40 seconds, an incredibly long time, and it was the type of run that cutters dream about. The cow surely tested the mare's ability, darting back and forth, pressing to get closer to the herd. Smart Date responded to the pressure by working even lower to the ground. At one point the cow stopped, completely mesmerized by the mare whose hindquarters quivered in anticipation. The mare forced the action by breaking into a rapid two-step, side to side.

The crowd was screaming, shouting, whistling, applauding at that point. The cow gave up and turned away. Leon raised his hand, lifting up the reins to take her off the cow. There were about 20 seconds left on the scoreboard clock, and he quickly skimmed another cow from the edge of the herd and was working when the buzzer sounded. The audience was wild with enthusiasm—this is what the aficionados had come to watch. Another loud round of applause followed the posting of three identical scores of 75 for a total of 225, which held up easily throughout the second section. Leon Harrel had added another victory to an already long line of wins for himself and his horses, and this one was worth more than $125,000 in prize money.

A crowd of reporters swarmed around him in the arena, shortly before the presentation of awards, and Leon told the group about Smart Date. She's by Smart Little Lena, who won the '82 Futurity, plus the '83 Derby and Super Stakes—cutting's triple crown. Her dam is Trip Date Bar; Smart Date is owned by Waltrip Ranches of Anderson, Texas.

Leon told how Bob Waltrip asked him early in the year to "go pick out a prospect we can win with, something that will put us right in the winner's circle." Leon spent two days looking at horses with Shorty Freeman, and "must have ridden 40 horses before deciding on this mare. She kind of fit me and Shorty knew it. She was kind of wild in the beginning, and he knew I've done well with that type. He encouraged us to buy her."

Leon noted that it was Shorty Freeman who initially broke Smart Date. "I want to point that out," he said, "because Shorty has been an inspiration and help to me for as long as I've been in the cutting business. He helped me get to my first futurity and gave me a lot of encouragement and confidence.

"And that's what I cultivated in the mare—confidence. I realized shortly after we had bought her that she had so much athletic ability, and so much desire in her, that what I had to do was continually work on her confidence in me. She had to learn that I wasn't going to hurt her, that she could count on me to not put her in a situation in which I would let her get hurt.

"She's the kind of mare that, when you walk by her stall, she nickers at you. She wants to be noticed, wants attention. She's small, and looking at her you wouldn't think she has all that power. But the mare is strong and has the heart and desire to excel. All this horse really needs at this point is just care, lots of care, keeping her healthy and feeling good. She's got the confidence to win."

Cutting has been Leon's lifeblood and livelihood ever since he became a full-time cutting horse trainer and contestant in 1968. Through the years he has become an integral part of the sport. He was an executive member of the NCHA from 1974 through '81, served as NCHA president in 1982, and is now a lifetime director and vice president. He has won consistently at the futurity since 1971, and that includes a previous first place in 1974. He rode Doc's Playmate to the NCHA world championship in 1978; that horse and another named Fizzabar that Leon had ridden years ago were both inducted into the NCHA Hall of Fame. Leon has also won virtually every futurity and maturity in NCHA competition, and picked up a couple of American Quarter Horse Association championships in cutting along the way.

Today he maintains an impressive training stable on his ranch near Kerrville, Tex., and he specializes in training young horses. He also has a keen interest in helping others learn how to ride and train cutting horses, and holds cutting clinics from time to time.

"Cutting has got to be one of the greatest sports we've ever come up with," he says. "There's nothing more natural than riding a cutting horse, and it's fun. Every member of the family can cut, and everyone can compete at whatever level of competition he or she is comfortable with. No one is forced into the mainstream of competition, but as people get better, they can gradually go to the next levels. They can go all the way to the open, against the open riders. There's no stopping place; there's a world of opportunity to show cutting horses.

"We have a lot of professional people in all types of business who cut on weekends for recreation, to be around horses and cattle, to be part of our great western heritage. We even have some people who are physically handicapped who ride cutting horses, and they do very well at it.

"It's so easy and so natural to learn if you get started off right with the proper kind of instruction, and get mounted on the proper horse. By that I mean a beginner doesn't want to start out on a horse that is too talented for him, so he falls off or gets scared. Beginners also need help in selecting and adjusting equipment.

"Cutting had some growing pains for a while, and was held back partly because it was considered a rich man's game, or something strictly for ranchers. But now, there are many places beginners can go to get help, horses aren't costing an arm and a leg, and people from all walks of life are discovering just how much fun this sport really is."

In the pages that follow, you're invited to learn more about cutting—how to ride, how to succeed in the sport, and how to train a horse to cut cattle. And you'll come to know more about Leon Harrel, a man with a homespun sense of humor, a good outlook on life, and a genuine affection for horses.

—Randy Witte

10

Presentation of awards at the 1987 NCHA Futurity: From left, Lance Harrel, Myrna Harrel (Leon's wife and Lance's mom), Bob Waltrip (owner of Smart Date), Smart Date and Leon Harrel, Denny Dunn, NCHA vice president, Shorty Freeman, and Jim Reno, NCHA president.
Photo by Pat Hall

2 How To Get Started

A beginner needs a good, honest show horse—a horse he or she is comfortable with and likes.

The NCHA

For people who want to get started in cutting: After reading this book, join the National Cutting Horse Association (NCHA). The NCHA is headquartered in Fort Worth and the mailing address is listed in the back of this book. As a member of the association, you'll receive the monthly NCHA magazine, *The Cuttin' Hoss Chatter*, which lists all the coming events and results of recent contests. You'll find out what competitions are coming up in your area of the country, what classes are available, and how much money is added.

Classes will vary a bit among shows, but a typical offering of classes includes the open (open to the world—the top cutters will be in this one), $10,000 non-professional (for those non-pro riders who haven't won more than $10,000), $3,000 novice (for those who have won less than $3,000), $1,500 novice, and youth (for riders 18 years of age and younger). Instead of a $3,000 novice, a show might have a $2,000 novice, or even a $500 novice; some shows have a class just for women, but on the whole, men and women compete on an equal basis.

Your NCHA membership benefits also include receiving the annual *Yearbook*, the *Rule Book*, the *Casebook* (which provides examples to further explain the rules), an NCHA decal, the right to participate in NCHA events and to vote in NCHA elections, the right to hold a non-pro card, and to take advantage of any corporate discounts made available to the NCHA. Membership fees are reasonable.

The NCHA also features a variety of age events: futurities for three-year-old horses, and maturities or derbies for four-, five-, and six-year-olds. Beginners typically need to stay with what we refer to as the weekend events, the events we described earlier, before jumping into these age events. There's more money involved with age events, and therefore tougher competition. So enter those weekend cuttings and get some experience, have some fun. As you become a better cutter, you'll naturally begin to seek higher levels of competition.

The NCHA each year recognizes a variety of champions and other top contenders, all determined on the basis of money won. These categories include the NCHA top ten cutting horses, top ten non-pro riders, top ten $10,000 limit non-pro riders, top ten youth, top ten $3,000 and $1,500 novice horses, and top ten open geldings. A champion stallion, mare, and gelding are also honored in the open division.

The richest, most prestigious event in the NCHA Championship Series is the World Championship Futurity, held the first couple weeks of December in Fort Worth, and featuring a purse of nearly $2 million. Hundreds of entries and thousands of spectators flock to Will Rogers Coliseum for this one, and there are a variety of horse sales, including an NCHA select sale of two-year-olds that are shown on cattle during the bidding. Many of these horses will return a year later to compete in the futurity—their first actual competition.

The World Championship Finals, with

I'm never at a loss for words when it comes to promoting cutting. This photo was snapped while I offered commentary at a celebrity roping and cutting.

a purse in excess of $100,000, is held in February during the Houston Livestock Show and Rodeo, and this one features the top 15 open and top 15 non-pro winners from the previous year.

The Affiliated and Area Workoff Championships are held each spring, and the top ten qualifiers in each of the various NCHA classes from each affiliate and area compete. Other prestigious contests, held in Fort Worth, include the Super Stakes and the Derby (both for four-year-old horses), the Super Stakes Classic (for five-year-olds), and the Breeders Cutting and NCHA Classic (both for four-year-olds). Participation in cutting overall has grown dramatically in recent years, and with that growth has come more corporate sponsorship and prize money. At this time, total prize money for all NCHA events is nearing $20 million a year.

The NCHA has been behind all this growth, and it has spilled into the American Quarter Horse Association (AQHA) and into youth rodeo. The National High School Rodeo Association has cutting among its rodeo events. I think a lot of youngsters start cutting there, just to pick up an extra event. Pretty soon, they're hooked on cutting. I can't give too much credit to the NCHA for the work it has done to promote cut-

ting, and to refine the rules and levels of competition. There are those who say cutting isn't a great spectator sport; well, there are long spells at each cutting when a new herd of cattle needs to be settled and the competition can't resume until the cattle are standing quietly at one end of the arena. But with the money up, and more exposure, continued growth is inevitable.

I don't mean to dwell on the money—people are attracted to the sport because they want to do something that involves horses and cattle and a western way of life. But it's nice to know that while cutting involves a certain financial commitment—buying a horse, perhaps paying training and boarding fees, and laying out money for equipment, travel expenses, and entry fees—there is a lot of opportunity to recoup those dollars. As people come up through the non-pro and open shows, they often go into the age events, where they can make quite a bit of money.

Buying a Horse

You need to get with someone you think is qualified to help find your first cutting horse. There are top cutters and trainers who will be glad to help, and they're located all around the country. Find someone you think will be honest with you, that you have some faith in, to help find a horse that will fit. What you want is a good honest show horse. I think it's also important that the rider is comfortable with the horse, not just the trainer or instructor. Don't buy a horse you don't like, for one reason or another, just because someone else says you should like him.

There are big horses that win, but I prefer a smaller horse. I don't like a horse bigger than 15 hands; I'd like that same horse better if he was 14.3. A bigger horse has to really get down in that dirt and declare himself when he turns; it's harder for him to present the same picture that a little smaller horse can show the judge. A smaller horse can just run over there and squat down, and look like he's really flat on the ground—a real working cutting horse. So I think it's easier to mark higher on the smaller horse. You can "steal" more on a small horse than you can win on a big one.

13

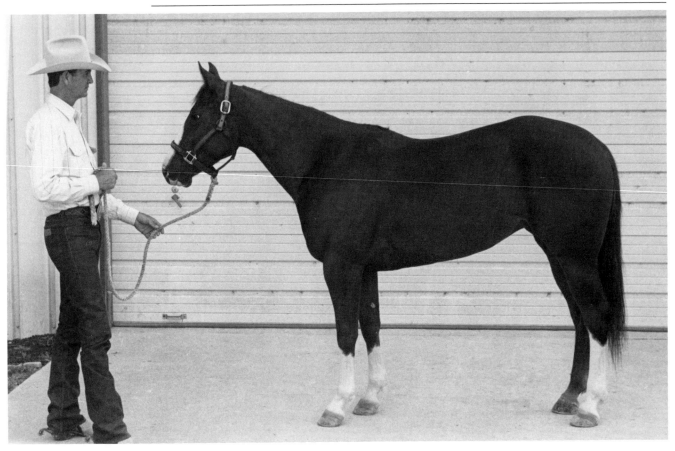

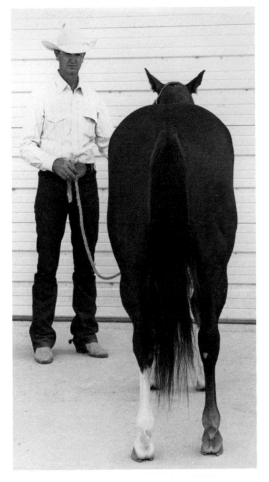

This is the mare, Smokin Spook Rio, that Lance is currently riding. She has the conformation I look for in a good cutting horse.

As far as bloodlines, these cutting horses can come from darn near anything. They're like race horses; they need to be well developed, but that winning edge has to come from desire, from wanting to please. I do think a person is smart, after he is really into cutting and begins to pay more money for horses, to stay with the real popular bloodlines. If you ever need to sell the horse or trade up, it's easier to get people interested in buying a popular bloodline than it is for a horse that is just "out of Oklahoma by Trailer." This is especially true of futurity horses—you can have an off-bloodline horse that looks great, but you can't get top dollar for him. Another horse will be from the popular bloodlines, and people will look at him all day.

Of course, the Doc Bar bloodlines are the greatest thing going, in my opinion, and most of the horses that are doing well have this lineage. They might be King Ranch horses crossed on the Doc Bar line, or Doc Bar horses crossed on something else, but it's nearly always there, somewhere. There are exceptions, but overall, the Doc Bar bloodlines have dominated the field for so long, they are really proven. Those horses are so

14

intelligent, so easy to work with.

Conformation: Everybody has their "rathers" here; they say horses with low hocks are going to be harder-stopping horses. And I think overall they are. I think it's easier for them to stop; but just because you have a horse that's not especially low hocked, or is straight in his hind legs, doesn't mean he won't stop. I've seen some straight-legged horses that were stopping son-of-a-guns. But, I would rather have a horse that is a little lower hocked if I'm looking to buy a two-year-old prospect.

I don't want a horse with a real long back; just an average back. I like a nice clean neck on a horse; and not real short. The horse should be well balanced. I like an attractive horse. You can win on an ugly horse, but I'll never go hunt one of them. I don't think color makes any difference in the picture you're presenting to a judge.

But . . .

But for beginners, it's not what the horse looks like, it's how that horse's performance fits you that is important. What kind of record does he have? Has he ever won anything? He's got to have some kind of performance record, unless he has been with one owner and was stuck off somewhere and hasn't had much opportunity to win. Chances are, however, if he doesn't have a record of winning something for someone, he's not for you. Make sure you ride the horse, try him out, and see how you like him. There has to be a bond, a harmony between horse and rider. In the show ring,

you're his silent partner; you'll be there to help him make his cuts, and to assist him through consistent, thoughtful riding. You've got to have confidence in one another, and that comes with time and practice.

When I talk about confidence, I think of the story about the old cowboy who woke up one morning and found himself in a hospital bed, and wearing a cast from head to toe. He glanced over and saw his buddy sitting there, and he asked him, "What in the world happened to me?"

"Well," says his buddy, "you remember last night we were playing cards in that third-floor hotel room, and you and I were losing to those other guys."

"Yeah, I remember."

"And those other fellas kept pourin' us plenty of whiskey to drink. . . ."

"I remember."

"Well, you finally bet 'em double or nothin' you could fly out that hotel window and run back up the stairs."

"My gawd!" he said. "And you let me actually jump out that window?"

"Let you?" says the buddy. "I bet another hundred that you could do it."

Now, that's showing real confidence. Not good judgment, in this instance, but real confidence.

3 EQUIPMENT

A variety of cutting saddles are on the market. Choose the one that feels best to you.

Saddles

For best results in cutting, a person must ride a cutting saddle. This type of saddle is built on a Buster Welch tree, named after the patriarch of the cutting horse world, the man who designed it many years ago. The tree is also referred to as a cutting tree. The result is a flat-seated saddle that isn't built up in front. Regular saddles that rise up in the front create a pocket for the rider to sit in next to the cantle. With the moves a cutting horse makes, the rider needs to be able to slide back and forth in the seat of that saddle. The cutter's free hand, the one

This standard cutting saddle is the one I use for showing. The saddle, breast collar, and headstall are trimmed with silver, and a thin, nice-looking saddle blanket is put on top of the regular saddle pad.

not holding the reins, grips the saddle horn—which is higher and thinner than other saddle horns, and therefore easier to hold—enabling the cutter to push and pull on it as the horse moves.

You need the freedom to move in the saddle so you can stay relaxed and stay down on the horse, just flowing with him; you'll move slightly forward and back in the saddle as he stops, turns, and moves in the opposite direction while working a cow. Don't try to just sit in one spot and think about screwing yourself into a rigid position; you're up there to be free and to float around as the horse moves—not to the point where you look sloppy, but to the point where the horse will jerk the saddle away from you, and you'll still be able to maintain that poise and composure you want to show the judge.

There can be some variation in how tall the fork is in the saddle, and therefore how high the horn sits. A lot of people with short arms like the tall forks, because they don't have to reach far to hold on. For those with long arms, it doesn't make any difference. There is also variation in how thick a horn is. Again, it's up to the rider; it's what feels best in his hand. I prefer the standard fork and horn.

The important thing about a saddle or any other equipment you choose is that it feels comfortable to you. You can get on one saddle and feel terrible, and try another and feel like you can ride a horse backwards and barefooted. That's how much difference a saddle can make.

These saddles resemble rodeo bronc-riding saddles in that the stirrups are very free moving, forward and backward. Most cutters today also use oxbow stirrups, or at least a *narrow* bell stirrup. The reason for this is the same reason oxbows are used in bronc riding—it's easier to keep your feet in this type of stirrup; you just don't lose a stirrup. It would be hard to ride a cutting horse and maintain much poise if you were trying to kick your foot back into a stirrup. For people who aren't used to riding with oxbows, I say you need to be aware of what you're doing when getting off a horse, so you don't hang up a foot.

Length of seat is very important in a cutting saddle. I would suggest a big person, with big thighs, would do well to get a 17-inch seat. I'm tall and lanky, and weigh 160 pounds, and a 16-inch seat is just right for me. Most people who make cutting saddles have done some cutting themselves, and will probably be able to help you select a saddle just by looking at you. But if the person in the saddle shop isn't sure what you need, and you're not sure, get a professional in there and ask him what size tree he would recommend for you. Never be afraid to ask for advice and opinions.

As for roughout, half roughout, or tooled saddles, it doesn't make any difference. That's strictly your choice. Most of these saddles have just a little bit of padding in the seat. Some people like the roughout, others prefer the plain leather seat that gets slightly slick through use. It's whatever feels best to you. Before you buy, you should try to ride another saddle just like it, or better yet, arrange to stick that very saddle on a horse. Most of the saddlemakers don't object to having someone put a new saddle on a horse in order to try it out. If you can't do that, however, at least sit in the saddle while it's on the rack, to see how it feels.

As for cinches, I prefer the wool, or soft synthetic-lined type, rather than mohair. These are easy to wash and they last a long time, and they add extra protection for the horses, minimizing the chances of galling or somehow damaging the muscles in the girth area. You do need to cinch up pretty tight when you go to cut.

I like to use a breast collar to help keep my saddle in place. Some horses don't need a breast collar, but it is sort of like insurance, I figure. If you don't get that cinch quite tight enough, and the horse really comes up and out of the ground hard, a breast collar will keep the saddle from slipping back. I don't want a breast collar adjusted very tight; just snugged up to the point where it's comfortable to the horse and won't interfere with his movements or his breathing.

Adjusting your stirrup length is very important. It's the real key to riding this saddle correctly. Sit in the saddle comfortably, just off the cantle maybe a half-inch (from spine to top of cantle), and put your feet all the way into the stirrups, right up to the heels. Sitting there like that, you should have a slight bend in your knees, enough so that when you straighten your legs, your hips slide back toward the cantle slightly, but don't quite touch it.

You know your stirrups are too long if you straighten your legs and there's no hip movement at all; they're too short if you straighten your legs and find yourself pushed against the cantle. If you ride with stirrups that are too long, when that horse moves across the arena and starts stopping, you'll straighten your knees and put a lot of weight on the bottom of your feet; your legs will be right down by his shoulder, creating an obstacle for him to turn around. With a slight bend in your legs, you'll get the support you need, and there won't be any obstacle for the horse; he'll be able to fold right over your leg and get out of the hole in that ground, so he can control the cow.

Saddle Blankets

I use a variety of blankets on different horses and for different types of riding. If I'm going to do a lot of riding on a horse, I'll use a blanket that has adequate protection for a horse's back, but is not so thick that it tends to roll. Thinner blankets that still offer plenty of good protection work best for fat-backed horses, because a thick pad or blanket will tend to roll. A thin or high-withered horse will need thicker padding. I like the blankets that look like a Navajo on the outside, but have the wool or fleece lining underneath. I also like wear leather strips on blankets.

I don't care to use the solid felt pads, especially in the summer, because they tend to sore a horse's back. If you had a softer blanket underneath this type of pad, that would probably work.

Take a look at your horse and the type of back he has. Don't use more padding than you need.

Bits

What we're trying to do with any bit (or with a hackamore or bosal, for that matter) is to control the horse and get him to do specific things. A bit is only as good as the person who is using it, and even a mild bit can be severe and hurt a horse's mouth if the rider starts yanking

on it. We'll discuss bits further in the training section, but for now I'll point out that I use a variety of snaffle bits for horses in training, and then go to shanked snaffles, like the Argentine, and various types of grazing bits. I like to keep as light a bit on a horse as I can for as long as possible. Some colts like to pack a little more iron and do better with a steel grazing bit, but I don't like to go to the real big, heavy bits. The port in the grazing bit will depend on the horse; some like a slightly high port, others like a low port. Regardless of the bit you're using, remember to have some compassion for the horse's mouth. When a person starts yanking on a horse's head, and the horse starts throwing his head and fighting the bit, head control is lost, and that means control of the horse is lost.

There are a few people who show horses in hackamores or bosals. I never have. I think it might even have a negative effect on some judges, to see a horse not bridled up. I prefer to stick with my bits.

Whatever kind of bit you use on a horse, it is important to know how that bit is supposed to be used, and how it is supposed to be adjusted. Most of the bits I put on horses will give them a slight "smile." One wrinkle, not too tight, yet not falling out of the mouth. This is the proper adjustment that can make the difference in whether a horse trains, and shows, well.

Reins

As for reins, I'll use fairly heavy, slightly thick reins ($5/8$- or $1/2$-inch wide) with a snaffle bit for training purposes, but as a rule I don't like exceptionally thick, heavy reins, especially for showing. A lot of it has to do with what feels comfortable in my hand. The reins should be adjusted so they feel balanced in your hand, a balance between the tail of the reins hanging down, and the length of reins from your hand to the bit. You need to adjust your reins so that when the horse is working there is enough slack in them so he doesn't bump himself in the mouth with the bit if he does something real hard. Some people like to show with reins hanging plumb down to the horse's knees; I don't think they have to be that long. Reins that

long also make it harder to control a
horse while cutting a cow from the herd.

Spurs

As a rule, a beginner shouldn't use
spurs, unless he's on an ol' dead-sided
horse that has to be spurred constantly
just to keep him going. And people with
short legs need to be careful about wearing spurs, even if they are experienced.
Short-legged folks have a tendency to
spur a horse without even knowing it
when they get a little tense, just because
of the proximity of the spurs to the
horse's sides. Wearing short-shanked
spurs helps prevent this. Long-legged
riders don't have to worry so much
about that, because their feet are hanging lower, away from the sides. The
main point here is to never spur a horse
accidentally. When a horse is spurred
and he doesn't need it, he'll quickly develop some bad habits. First thing you
know, he's jumping out of his turns and
being too aggressive with cattle; he's
becoming what we call a charging horse.

Protective Gear

Young horses in training, seasoned
horses in the practice pen, and most all
cutting horses in competition should
have at least a minimum of protective
gear on their legs to help prevent injury
to themselves while working a cow. By
minimum I mean a combination boot on
the front and back legs that protects the
area from just below the knees or hocks
down over the fetlocks. If a horse hits a
splint bone and gets sore, or strikes himself anywhere else around his legs, he
simply won't train or show to his potential. If he burns the fetlocks on his hind
legs in a hard stop, he'll simply quit stopping hard.

*Protective boots for front legs (top), and
hind legs.*

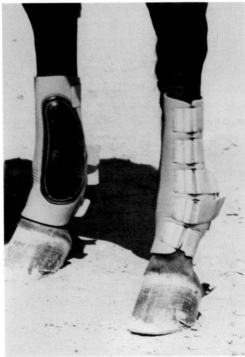

4 HOW TO RIDE

Follow these few simple rules for riding, and you'll just blend into the action.

Stay Relaxed

To ride a cutting horse, you need to stay relaxed in the hips and lower back. We call that the cutter's slump. Sit slightly off the cantle, with stirrups adjusted so you're not pushed up tight against the cantle when you straighten your legs. It helps to think about sitting on your back pockets; let your lower back bend, and just scoot those pockets right under yourself. As the horse moves, you'll take most of the shock from the stops and turns in your back and hip area. To keep from going forward, push on the saddle horn. When the horse gets up to go after that cow, pull on the horn. That's how you main-

The cutter's slump—lower back is relaxed and bent, heels are down, free hand is on the saddle horn, rein hand is down in front of the saddle, and my eyes are on the cow being worked.

Pull on the horn when the horse is trying to get out of that ground, coming out of a turn.

Push on the horn and sit deep in the saddle to help the horse in a stop. Remember to keep your heels down.

tain that posture, by constantly pushing and pulling on the horn.

If a person sits up too straight, becomes too rigid, the tendency will be to lean left or right. Maintaining the correct seat lets you really be a part of the horse. Your left hand (or whichever hand is holding the reins) will be held quietly down on top of the horse's neck, not necessarily touching the horse, but immediately in front of the saddle, and it will stay there until you are through working a cow. That horse can go anywhere, and you'll just be low in the saddle and go with him, left or right. You won't have a lot of pressure in your stirrups, just enough so your feet are comfortable and feel secure. *Keep your heels down, lower than your toes. This will prevent your feet from slipping back, and your body from being thrown forward.*

This is the posture the judges look for—it's a poised, confident look, a winning look. You'll be able to maintain a low center of gravity and just flow and move with him. It's very easy to do this, if you'll remember just one more thing: *Keep your eyes on the cow.*

If you watch the cow, concentrate on the cow, you'll blend right into the whole picture. Don't look down at the horse. If you look down, your riding will become difficult immediately, because the horse will make some moves that you don't see coming. If you're adjusting to him, rather than the cow, you'll be behind the action; you'll become rigid, and find yourself off to one side or the other. Watch the cow—where the cow goes, the horse will go, and you'll just blend into the action. Cow, horse, and rider will all be in harmony.

Some people start anticipating too

much. They'll lean one direction or the other, and do what we call "drop a shoulder." When they do that, their weight is on one side or the other, instead of the middle of the saddle. A lot of times the horse will try to get back under that weight, and he'll do things like move toward the cow, round the turns off, and not run or stop properly. React to what you see so you can move with the horse, but don't anticipate a move that hasn't occurred. You're just there to go for the ride, and to assist the horse if he needs it after you've made that cut. You assist the horse by staying down in the saddle, and pushing or pulling on the horn so the horse isn't just packing dead weight.

Now that we've talked about the basics of riding a cutting horse, let's get into the role your help plays in order for you to show your horse. Let's talk our way through an imaginary 2½-minute run (cutting exhibition) that you're about to make.

Bring In the Cattle

The NCHA recommends that there are 2½ head of cattle for every horse entered in a go-round. The cattle are divided evenly into groups, with no more than 15 cutters working a single bunch of cattle. The cutters draw for working order, and if there are 15 cutters in the first group, that means they will take turns working a herd of at least 37 head of cattle. If there are, say, 12 cutters, then they will work at least 30 head of cattle. The cattle will be traded for a fresh bunch before the next group begins to cut.

The reason for changing cattle so often is that cattle quickly sour on cutting. A fresh cow is most likely to stay in the middle of the arena and really challenge a horse, trying to get back to the herd. A cow that has just been cut and worked once or twice is more likely to give up, not try as hard to get back to the herd; or may just run back and forth across the arena, or simply try to run past the turnback men and head for the opposite end of the arena. You can't show your horse's ability very well on a cow that does that. NCHA rules state that if there aren't enough fresh cattle for both open and non-pro classes, and if purses, entry

fees, and cattle charges are equal in both divisions, then a coin is tossed to see which class gets to use the cattle first. NCHA-approved shows with youth classes are always urged to provide fresh cattle for that category.

Settling the Herd

When a fresh bunch of cattle are brought into the arena, they need to be settled. All this means is that the cattle are conditioned to stay bunched, just inside the in-gate, and to not scatter when a horse is moving back and forth near the edge of the herd. This can be done, in anywhere from 20 to 40 minutes or so, by several riders. Two riders, acting as herd holders, will stay in proximity to the cattle on each side, to prevent them from moving up one side of the fence or the other; the cattle aren't crowded, they're just held in the area we want them.

A third rider then walks, trots, and lopes back and forth in front of the herd, simulating the movements of a cutting horse at work. The cattle will be skittish at first, but gradually calm down. At that point the "cutter" will ride into the herd, quietly drive out a bunch of cattle, and let them walk back to the herd.

For cattle that are fairly wild to begin with, it will help to have some other cutters sitting horseback out in the arena, acting as passive turnback riders. There will be more loping in front of the herd, and more cattle will be driven out into the arena and allowed to return to that area next to the gate in which they feel comfortable. Once the cattle are settled, we're ready to cut.

Turnback Riders and Herd Holders

Cutting for practice and cutting in competition are different in some respects. You don't always need a full force of turnback riders and herd holders in practice, which we'll discuss in the chapter on training. But at a cutting contest, a person needs to get the best help he can find. Most of the top cutters haul what we refer to as turnback horses, in addition to their cutting horses. In other words, a cutting horse in competition usually doesn't help hold herd or turn back cattle. Cutting and turning back are two separate jobs, and the cutting horse doesn't need the extra work and pressure. A turnback horse might be an older cutting horse that isn't shown anymore, or he might be an all-around horse that's used for a variety of chores around home.

Cutters always help one another, and when you go to a cutting you should ask assistance from people you think can help you win. I don't care if you ask Buster Welch or Matlock Rose or Leon Harrel; if these people don't have a conflict in their schedules, i.e., they're about to compete themselves, they'll be glad to help you as a turnback man or herd holder. If another cutter says he will help, you can be sure he'll do whatever he can to assist your run. That's just the way it is in this sport.

Once you have your help lined up, communicate to them. Ask their opinions of the cattle: Are there any cows they really like the looks of? Have they seen any you should avoid? As you come along in cutting, you'll also learn how your horse works best. You might say, "Hey, this horse is a little chargey (wants to push a cow down the arena rather than merely prevent her from returning to the herd). I want you turnback men to move in on us; put some heat on this horse. Don't let him get out of there."

Or you might have a horse that you can say this about him: "Boys, this horse has a lot of pretty moves and handles a cow good by himself. You guys sort of stay back and stay wide, and just stop cattle on those hard runs, but let me handle it."

And yes, a herd holder can help turn a cow back that is running hard toward his side of the area if your cutting horse is having trouble catching and turning her. He does this by riding between his end of the herd and the cow.

In this case, you've probably already lost a point for losing the working advantage (your horse is too far behind the cow to turn her), and you may lose two points for letting her get to the back fence (either side of the herd), but that's better than losing five points for letting the cow get back into the herd. Ideally, the cutting horse should travel parallel to the cow, and slightly behind; the horse's head should be about even with the cow's shoulder. This is what we mean by working advantage.

The herd holders are there basically to help shape up the cattle and drive them out into the arena as you're making your cut. They can help move cattle out of the way once it's obvious you're not trying to cut one of them, so you can start "clean" with a cow, with no other cattle in the way. After you've made your cut they'll move back to their areas, and watch the herd. If a cow tries to get out

Making a deep cut, coming in behind the herd, pushing the cattle out into the center of the arena.

23

1/ A cut from the side of the herd. I'll move behind these cattle and drive them away from the others.

2/ Cattle drift back on both sides of us. I'll pick the calf that stops and looks at us.

3/ This is the one we'll work. We're stepping to the right to stop this calf and begin our work.

1/ Horse and cutter are both relaxed, making this cut. This is what you want.

2/ The remaining three calves suddenly break and run. A person doesn't want to cut on the run, if he can avoid it, but sometimes you can't avoid it.

3/ This shows how we moved out with the cattle and cut the angle back to the herd by pressing off (away) from the last calf. We get the calf stopped; in fact the calf is already beginning to turn back the other way.

By maintaining the correct posture and concentrating on the cow, you'll become one with the horse and just flow with the action. Relax and enjoy it—the saddle is the best seat in the house!

sage to your horse, and then he'll become apprehensive or nervous. Horses are that sensitive. They can feel subtle leg pressure, they can feel nervousness through the reins. And a horse that becomes nervous because the rider is nervous is prone to make a mistake. It's like playing poker; you can be dealt a winning hand, and you feel so excited you want to grin. But you can't even show a hint of excitement in your eyes. Same way with cutting. Keep everything quiet and relaxed, and you'll get off to a good start.

Okay, your herd holders and turnback riders are in place. Now walk your horse on down to the herd. You'll cross a marker on the side of the fence—the time line—and the clock will start running. Rule one says each horse is required to make at least one deep cut. This means at some point—either on your first cut or your second—you need to actually ride into the herd and drive out at least three head of cattle, rather than simply cutting out a cow on the edge. I like to bring out at least eight or ten head—it looks better to a judge. Most people make their first cut deep, to make sure the rule is satisfied while there's plenty of time.

You can legally quit working a calf when the calf is either stopped, or is turned away from you, and either moving or not moving. Signal the horse to stop by raising your rein hand.

Another way to signal a properly trained cutting horse to stop working is to take your hand off the saddle horn and place it firmly on the horse's neck. I've done this when I wanted to make sure I wouldn't get caught for a hot quit; if I wanted to resume working that cow—if the cow turned back suddenly, or was facing me and suddenly moved before I could raise my hand—my rein would still be down and I wouldn't be penalized. If I was sure I wanted to quit, I could go ahead and raise my rein hand, and go back to the herd.

Enter the herd from any position—middle, left side, right side, or from the back—and drive some cattle out of there (maybe five or six head or more), and take them straight up the middle of the arena. The herd holders will help push the cattle forward. Rather than try to cut a particular cow, you decide to cut for "shape." That means you'll let the cattle flow back around on either side, and maybe step the horse toward the last several head, stopping them, and then picking the cow that looks like she'll give you the best working advantage. Maybe two cows will walk off together to one side, and the third one hesitates and looks at you. That's the one to work.

At this point your free hand is on the saddle horn, and your rein hand is still up. You can keep your hand up to cue the horse and move with the cow a few steps one way or another if necessary, if you still have cattle that are not behind you. It's best not to start on the run; you want the cow standing still when you lower your rein hand to begin working. Take as little time as necessary to get the cow shaped up, then lower your hand to the horse's neck, just in front of the saddle, and keep it there. Lowering the reins tells the horse and the judge that you're ready to begin. You'll be thinking left or right, no more forward motion.

Let's say the cow bolts to your left. You'll instinctively pull on the saddle horn and apply a little pressure in the right stirrup, and some leg pressure on the right side of the horse. Maintaining the cutter's slump, you see the cow stop and turn toward the horse to move in the opposite direction. You automatically maintain that deep seat in the saddle and push against the horn. The horse comes up from the ground, your eyes stay on the cow, and you pull on the saddle horn, instinctively applying some pressure with your foot in the left stirrup, while your left leg moves against the horse's left side.

The cow gives you a pretty good challenge, and at one point your horse is really dominating her, stepping left and right, back and forth. You feel the saddle sort of floating back and forth, side to side, and think about sitting on your pockets with your back relaxed. It feels so good you want to grin, but just keep watching the cow.

Suddenly, the cow just throws up her head and trots toward the opposite end of the arena. She's probably given her best effort; she'll be more inclined to run off with more work, and won't add any more to the performance. You raise your hand to quit while she's still moving away.

The 2½ minutes is clicking off in your mind, and you know there is ample time to cut another cow. Don't spin your horse around and rush back to the herd. Instead, pause to check the bridle reins, to make sure they're not tangled. The tail of one rein hanging over a rein to the bit might confuse the horse. Reach down and straighten the reins, then step over to the herd and look at the cattle. Run a quick mental check on yourself: Are you relaxed or are you getting tense? If you're tense, take a deep breath and think "relax." Then make another cut.

Time's running and you figure maybe it isn't necessary to make another deep cut; there are a couple heifers standing on the edge of the herd that look good. Ride over and skim them off the edge and push them into the middle of the arena. Make sure you get behind them so you can drive them away from the herd.

You wind up taking the cow that gives you the best working advantage, a cow that's turned around and is looking at you. The other one slips on by to return to the herd, and you take a step to prevent the one you want from following. Your free hand grips the saddle horn again while your rein hand drops back down to the horse's neck. You're working this cow and find she's not quite as good as the first one; there's more running and stopping from side to side, and then she runs toward the turnback men.

At home, you've practiced judging the 2½ minutes in your mind, and figure you don't have that much time left to get off of this cow and make a third cut, so you decide to keep working this one, rather than "die in the herd" (be bringing out more cattle rather than actually working a cow when the buzzer sounds). There's nothing technically wrong with that, but it always looks better to be working right up to the end. At the major cuttings, there's usually a clock to glance at; and one of your helpers can call out "15 seconds" or whatever is left on the clock. But the weekend cuttings don't have a clock.

The turnback riders see that you want to continue working this cow if possible, so they stop the cow and turn her back toward you. Your horse is working the cow when the buzzer sounds, signalling the end of your competition.

When you raise your hand to quit, the look on your face tells everyone who was watching, "That's just the way I wanted it to go."

5 JUDGING AND SCORING

Whether a cutting has one judge or as many as five, each judge scores from 60 to 80 points.

Rules for Judging Cutting Horse Contests

1/ Each horse is required to enter the herd sufficiently deep enough to show his ability to make a cut. One such deep cut will satisfy this rule. Failure to satisfy this requirement will result in a three (3) point penalty.

a/ A horse *will* be given credit for his ability to enter the herd quietly with very little disturbance to the herd or to the one brought out.

2/ When an animal is cut from the herd, it is more desirable that it be taken toward the center of the arena, and credit *will* be given for same. Additional credit *will* be given the horse that drives its stock sufficient distance from the herd to assure that the herd will not be disturbed by his work; thereby showing his ability to drive a cow.

3/ Credit *will* be given for riding with a loose rein throughout a performance.

4/ Credit *will* be given for setting up a cow and holding it in a working position as near the center of the arena as possible.

5/ If the cutting horse or his rider creates disturbance at any time throughout his working period, he will be penalized:

a/ Any noise directed by the contestant toward the cattle will be penalized one (1) point.

b/ Each time a horse runs into the herd, scatters the herd while working, or picks up cattle through fault of the horse, he will be penalized three (3) points.

c/ The judge shall stop any work because of training or abuse of his horse by the contestant or disturbance of the cattle. Any contestant failing to stop immediately will be penalized $500, payable to NCHA prior to entry in any other NCHA-approved event.

6/ A horse will be penalized three (3) points each time the back fence actually stops or turns the animal being worked within one step of the fence; the back fence to be agreed on and designated by the judge or judges before the contest starts; meaning the actual fence only, no imaginary line from point to point to be considered. If any of the contestants voice an objection before the contest starts, the judge or judges shall take a vote of the contestants, and a "back fence" acceptable to the majority shall be designated and used.

7/ If a horse turns the wrong way with tail toward animal being worked, an automatic score of 60 points will be given.

8/ While working, a horse will be penalized one (1) point each time the reins are used to control or direct (to rein) the horse, regardless of whether the reins are held high or low. A one (1) point penalty shall also be charged whenever a horse is visibly cued in any manner. If the reins are tight enough that the bit is bumped at any time, he shall be penalized one (1) point each time even though the hand of the rider does not move.

a/ A horse must be released as soon as the desired animal is clear of the other cattle. Additional reining, cueing, or positioning will result in a one (1) point penalty for each occurrence.

b/ The rider shall hold the bridle reins in one hand. A three (3) point penalty shall be charged if the second hand touches the reins for any purpose except to straighten them while the horse is: (1) approaching the herd to make a cut or (2) is completely stopped within the body of the herd or (3) to retrieve a rein that has been dropped after completely stopping the horse.

c/ Spurring behind the shoulder shall not be considered a visible cue. A three (3) point penalty shall be assessed each time a horse is spurred in the shoulder.

d/ A toe, foot, or stirrup on the horse's shoulder is considered a visible cue. A one (1) point penalty shall be charged for each occurrence.

9/ If a horse lets an animal that he is working get back in the herd, he will be penalized five (5) points.

10/ If a rider changes cattle after visibly committing to a specific cow, a five (5) point penalty will be assessed.

11/ When a horse goes past an animal to the degree he loses his working advantage, he will be penalized one (1) point each time he does so.

12/ Unnecessary roughness, such as a horse actually pawing, biting, or kicking cattle, will be penalized three (3) points.

13/ A contestant may quit an animal when it is obviously stopped, obviously turned away, or is obviously behind the turnback horses *and the turnback horses are behind the time line.* A penalty of three (3) points must be charged if the animal is quit under any other circumstances.

14/ If a horse quits a cow, a penalty of five (5) points will be assessed.

15/ If a horse clears the herd with two (2) or more cattle and fails to separate a single animal before quitting, a five (5) point penalty will be charged. There is no penalty if time expires.

16/ Horses must be ridden with a bridle having a bit in the mouth or with a hackamore. A bridle shall have no noseband or bosal and hackamores shall be of rope or braided rawhide with no metal parts. A judge must be able to freely pass two fingers between the hackamore and muzzle completely around the horse's nose. Choke ropes, tie-downs, wire around the horse's neck, nose, or browband, tight noseband, quirt, bat, or mechanical device giving the rider undue control over a horse will not be permitted in the arena where an NCHA-approved or -sponsored event is being held. Breast collar may be used, no portion of which may pass over the horse's neck. Chaps and spurs may be worn. Anytime a contestant is guilty of an infraction of this rule or any part therein, he shall be disqualified. A judge has the right to have a contestant report to him if he's suspicious of any infraction of Rule 16.

a/ All horses must comply with Rule 16 while in the arena.

b/ Any person in the arena after the start of an NCHA-approved or -sponsored event must wear western attire, including hats. Men must wear long-sleeved shirts with collars and buttons or snaps completely down the shirt front. T-shirts and slipover knits are not permissible. Women must wear long-sleeved shirts with a collar. Sweaters may be worn over an appropriate shirt.

c/ Rule 16 shall become effective one (1) hour prior to the published starting time of championship and jackpot cuttings. At limited age events and other special events approved by the NCHA, Rule 16 shall become effective three (3) hours prior to the published starting time each day and shall remain in effect until one hour after each day's performance is concluded.

d/ Rule 16 may be set aside by show management for an official practice session provided that the practice session ends at least one hour prior to the start of any performance.

e/ If an officer, director, or duly elected or appointed contestant's representative of the NCHA witnesses a violation of standing Rule 16, they must report the violation immediately to the association executive director.

f/ Violations of Rule 16 shall result in: First offense—$200 fine; Second offense—$500 fine; Third and subsequent offenses within 12 months—90-day suspension.

17/ When a contestant is thrown from a horse or horse falls to ground, an automatic score of sixty (60) points will be given.

18/ Any rider who allows his horse to quit working or leave the working area before his allotted time is up will be disqualified for that go-round with no

Five judges, isolated from one another on platforms (top of photo), watch Buster Welch cut a cow at the NCHA Futurity. Buster's horse, incidentally, shows excellent position on this calf.

score.

19/ A contestant will be awarded a complete rework if, in the judge or judges' opinion, 2½ minutes time was not allotted for the work, or if excessive disturbances had been created by factors other than those caused by the contestants or their help and the judge or judges have stopped the time. Such factors would include gates coming open, fences falling down, and objects entering or falling into the working portion of the arena, but would not apply to cattle scattering through wildness or normal arena activities. Any rework must take place within the group of cattle drawn by the contestant and must occur before a change of cattle is executed. At the contestant's option, the rework may occur immediately or as the last work in that set of cattle. No rework shall be granted if the contestant involved has incurred a five (5) point (major) penalty prior to a disturbance. If, in the cutter's opinion, a situation has occurred of sufficient seriousness so as to warrant a rerun, he may immediately make a request for the same to the contestant's representative or to the designated equipment judge who shall report this fact to show management before the next horse is called to work. Show management shall make such facts as are available known to the judge(s) and, if they are unanimous in agreement that due cause did exist, a rerun may be granted provided the original work was free of a five (5) point (major) infraction.

20/ A judge marks from sixty (60) to eighty (80) points. One-half (½) points are permissible.

21/ When the judge is in doubt about a penalty, the benefit always goes to the contestant.

Reprinted with permission from National Cutting Horse Association Rule Book. Be sure to check the latest NCHA Rule Book for any rule changes.

How Scoring Works

Whether a cutting has one judge or as many as five judges, each judge scores the same, from 60 to 80 points. At the beginning of each run, a judge will typically picture an average score of 70 in his mind, and as the work progresses, he can either add points (giving credit for herd work, for driving a cow, setting up a cow to begin work, riding with loose reins, working in the center of the arena, and the degree of difficulty or challenge presented to the cutter), or he can deduct points for whatever he sees lacking in the run content. When the work is finished, the judge totals whatever penalty points were incurred, if any, and he deducts those points from the overall score he determined. The final score is written on his judges' card, and at the end of that go-round the show management is required to post his markings. If more than one judge is judging a cutting, neither is allowed to consult with the other until after the cards are turned in, and no markings may be changed once the cards are turned in.

The NCHA has an excellent judging system and judge monitoring program. Judges are allowed to advance from an A rating, to AA, and finally to AAA. Naturally, the AAA judges are eligible to officiate at the richest cuttings. The NCHA also has a very comprehensible *Rule Book* and a *Casebook* that supplements the rules by further explaining all the fine points of judging and showing. The result is a successful effort to allow everyone in the association the opportunity to correctly interpret every rule and to understand how a judge evaluates a run. Both the *Rule Book* and *Casebook* are sent to every member at the beginning of each year.

The first thing a judge looks at, of course, is the herd work. He wants to see a horse either walk or trot toward the herd on a light rein, and to pull up enough so he doesn't disturb the herd as he enters it. He doesn't want to see the horse or rider show any hesitation about entering the herd. To satisfy the rule for making at least one deep cut in the herd,

the book says the cutter simply has to "go deep enough to show his ability to get one out." If I'm a contestant, I like to bring out at least six or eight head of cattle so there's no doubt that I made a deep cut.

It's fine to keep your rein hand up, and to cue the horse with your reins while you're separating one cow from all the others, but as soon as the rest of the cattle are moved back, the cutter should put his hand down at that point, and not pick it up again or give any other visible cue (including waving or shouting) until he is done working that cow. The one thing you can do is use leg cues, as long as you don't spur in front of the cinch.

After the first cow is worked, the judge will have a pretty good idea of what's going on. If the cow tried that horse pretty good, and the horse was running and stopping good, and the horse maintained good working advantage, the judge evaluates this and may move him up to 71 or 72 or 73 points. As the cutter goes back in the herd for another cut, the evaluation continues. He doesn't have to make a deep cut this time, but again, it should be done quietly, without disturbing the cattle. If the cutter is free of penalties after the second cut, the judge will have to decide whether that second cow added anything to the run.

The rules state that no more than three cows may be cut if the cattle are fresh. Is cutting three better than two? Not necessarily. The one who cut two cows may have done more actual work than another who cut three. The judge evaluates this too. Did the cutter look like he was spending too much time in the herd? Did he appear timid or did he show a lot of courage, perhaps staying on a tough cow that was really testing his horse?

A horse can lose working advantage on a cow either while both horse and cow are in motion, or when a cow makes a move after standing still. (A horse may have to lose working advantage by running far enough ahead of the cow to get her to turn, and the cow turns and the horse is left behind.) But credit is given if that horse is able to turn and catch up to

NCHA JUDGES CARD

Event _____

Go Round _____

CREDIT:

Herd Work
Driving a Cow
Setting up a Cow
Loose Reins
Working Center of Arena
Degree of Difficulty
Amount of Working Time
Amount of Courage

PENALTIES:

(a) 1 point - (miss) losing working advantage (11)
(b) 1 point - reined or visibly cued (8)
(c) 1 point - noise directed to cattle (5a)
(d) 1 point - toe, foot or stirrup on the shoulder (8d)

(a) 3 points - hot quit (13)
(b) 3 points - cattle picked up or scattered (5b)
(c) 3 points - second hand on reins (8b)
(d) 3 points - spur in shoulder (8c)
(e) 3 points - pawing or biting cattle (12)
(f) 3 points - failure to make deep cut (1)
(g) 3 points - back fence (6)

(a) 5 points - horse quitting a cow (14)
(b) 5 points - losing a cow (9)
(c) 5 points - changing cattle after a
    specific commitment (10)
(d) 5 points - failure to separate a single
    animal after leaving the herd (15)

60 - if horse turns tail (7)
60 - if horse falls to ground (17)

Disqualification (score 0) - illegal
    equipment or leaves working
    area before time expires

HORSE	SCORE	PENALTIES			CREDITS			
		1 PT	3 PTS	5 PTS	Herd Work	Setting up a Cow	Degree of difficulty	Eye Appeal

Courtesy of
National Cutting Horse Association

Judge's Signature _____

the cow, regaining the working advantage, with his head at the cow's shoulder. If a cow is standing still and suddenly moves to one side or the other, and the horse is caught "flat-footed" and gazing off to the side of the arena, he'll lose a point if he loses working advantage, even if he is able to catch up to the cow and turn her before she gets back to the herd. If the rider had to raise his hand to cue the horse into motion, another penalty point will be assessed.

The judge is also evaluating the horse's ability to drive a cow from the herd when making a cut. The work should be done far enough away from the herd so the herd isn't disturbed. Credit is also given for driving a cow straight up the middle of the arena, rather than off to one side, when making the cut from the herd.

Rounding out the picture, the judge is looking for a professional look overall— good riding, a still hand on the reins. Saddle and bridle don't have to be fancy, but they should be properly adjusted, neat, and clean; and the same goes for the rider's clothing. A judge may mark a clean, penalty-free run 72 or 72½ points, at least. If he's really impressed, he may mark the cutter 73 or 74. If the content of the run was definitely above average, he'll probably score it even higher.

The back-fence penalty may need a bit more explanation. The back fence is a designated area on the fence behind the cattle. A cutter is penalized three points each time the cow reaches within one step, or three feet, of that area.

Another rule that may need more clarification concerns "picking up cattle." If another cow enters the working area while the cutter is still working the cow he cut, no penalty is assessed unless the judge determines that the cutter was too close to the herd and disturbed it. If the judge determines the cutter was at fault, and caused the extra cow to leave the herd and get "picked up," then he'll penalize the cutter three points.

As I mentioned in the last chapter, it doesn't matter technically if you "die in the herd" when the buzzer sounds; in other words, when you're in the process of making another cut. But when I'm competing, I try to always be actually working a cow when the buzzer sounds. I just think it looks better; it's preferable. But a good judge won't penalize anyone just because he or she wasn't working a cow right up to the end.

6 CATTLE

General information on their care; characteristics of various breeds.

To be consistent with terminology, I've been referring to the cattle we cut as cows, but as I mentioned early in the book, it's just as proper to refer to them as calves. The cattle are actually not always cows or heifers, either. Most of the weekend cuttings will have mixed cattle—steers as well as heifers. The major events, particularly the age events, will invariably have all heifers, though, because heifers show more action, they're livelier, present more of a challenge to a horse, than do steers. If I'm cutting from a herd of mixed cattle, I'll usually try to cut a heifer for that reason, unless the heifers are just plain wild acting, and are doing a lot of running. Then I may look for a steer. If time's running out and I'm trying to make another cut and see a couple steers at the edge of the herd, I may go ahead and take a steer just because he's handy, and because steers are usually more gentle than heifers, and therefore easier to cut. Generally speaking, heifers make better cattle for cutting, either for practice or competition, because they're livelier than steers.

For some of the major age events, the people who supply the cattle will have specific guidelines they'll start to follow many months ahead of time. They'll supply perhaps 3,000 head of heifers, all uniform in weight and type. The cattle will be brought in in bunches that are all from the same herd, which helps in settling them. In the age events, we work the best cattle possible. At the weekend cuttings, however, we can be cutting anything. So it helps to learn general

characteristics about cattle in order to size up a herd and pick the type of calf you want, or at least avoid the calves you spot beforehand that seem likely to cause you a problem.

If you're looking to buy maybe several head of cattle to keep at home for practice, heifers will last longer than steers before they go sour on cutting, and stop giving you the type of work you need. Cattle sour very quickly, and as we discussed earlier, that means they'll simply choose to no longer play the game, or do nothing more than run back and forth across the arena. You can keep cattle working the longest, however, if you never work one until she's tired, and if you provide plenty of water, feed, and adequate shelter. Older cattle are better than young cattle, because they aren't as prone to get sick. Large-boned heifers, that are at least yearlings and are gaining weight, are the best. With good care and light use, they can provide adequate practice for a number of weeks. But it seems like you can never get enough cattle, because they do sour on the game in a relatively short time. Getting a mechanical cow (and there are several of these on the market) is an alternative, but there's no substitute, in my opinion, for live cattle.

The area in which you live will pretty much determine what type of cattle you use, as far as training and tuning up your horse for showing. I think the best cattle you can train with or tune a horse with are the English breeds, like Hereford, Angus, and Hereford-Angus crosses (black baldies). The English breeds are

A variety of cattle, including Hereford, Hereford-Angus (black baldy) crosses, and Brahma crosses.

gentle. They give you more time to show your horse, more time to place the horse, more time to stop, more time to make the cut, more time to work on your riding, to work on yourself. They aren't as fast as other breeds, or crossbred cattle with Brahma in them. And they last quite a while before they get sour, as long as they're cared for properly.

I'm fortunate to live in an area where I have access to a lot of fresh cattle, and I trade cattle constantly. We use a lot of crossbred cattle, and they're sprinkled with some English cattle. This works good for me. If I have a colt that needs a lot of time, or a horse that just needs certain maneuvers polished up, I can cut one of the softer calves and have more time. Then if I want to test a horse a bit, I can cut something that's faster. I like to bring in a hundred head of cattle, and maybe put about 20 in the arena, and keep the rest in pens back behind. They'll have water, feed, and shade, and when I get done working the first 20, we turn them back to the pens so they can rest, and then bring up another 20 or so.

Brahma crosses—and we have a lot of this type in my part of Texas—will be a lot more difficult to handle compared to the English breeds. Just driving them up from the pens will take more time; you need to ease these cattle around, not push them, to keep from making them wilder. They're harder to settle when they're fresh, and they'll run more; they'll just give you less time to do everything you need to do. They're harder to cut out of the herd; they're quick, tricky. The fewer straight Brahmas or Brahma crosses a beginner has to work, the better off he'll be. A lot of your other crossbred cattle can be pretty good to work, but they have to be handled gently at first. Anyway, you'll end up cutting both English and crossbred cattle, including Brahmas, at the cutting competitions.

When cutting a Brahma, the important thing is to get him out of the herd slowly, gently, and catch him standing still and cleaned up (no other cattle milling around) before you start working. If he starts moving around and you've still got a lot of cattle out there, he's proba-

When the cattle aren't being used, they've got adequate shade, water, and feed.

Moving up the alley-way, into the holding pens; I like to take it easy with them, and not bring the cattle in on the run.

Into the round pen. The herd will be settled on the side or in the middle, depending upon the type of horse training I've scheduled.

bly going to get harder to cut. If you can get him standing flat-footed and relaxed, he will probably turn around and play you pretty good for a while. And once you hit him five or six licks, and he starts running back and forth, then look for an opportunity to get off of him—because he'll probably end up trying to run over you.

As I said, I have good access to cattle. We get in a hundred head every two weeks. But a lot of these guys use a hundred head every three or four days—that's one reason a horse trainer has trouble making any money! Cattle expense is tremendous. But a person working on his own, with just his own horse, can do very well with a few head of cattle on hand, if the cattle are given good care and handled properly.

If you're working with just one cow in a round pen (which will be discussed in the chapter on training), there is no need to try to settle that cow. If you're working with a few head or a regular herd of cattle, always take the time to settle them at one end of the arena or a particular place in the pen. If you don't take the time to do this, you'll stir them up, they'll start running, and you'll ruin that bunch of cattle for cutting before you even get started.

At a show, it's hard for people to pick cattle to cut if they haven't spent a lot of time with cattle, and that's why we talked about cutting for shape (picking the last cow that gives you the best opportunity to cut) versus cutting an individual (maneuvering and sorting cattle until you get the individual you want). But what beginners should look for are cattle that appear to be gentle. When the herd is being settled, and you look down there and see some cattle that are doing a lot of running back and forth, you know you won't want to intentionally cut one of them. Make a mental note of any distinguishing characteristics, so you can recognize them when you're going into the herd.

There will probably also be cattle in that bunch that you notice will walk out there and don't overreact to the guy who is settling them. They won't do a lot of running; they'll acknowledge the horse, but won't be acting wild. They'll move slower; when they get out in front of the herd, they won't try to immediately get back and hide in the herd.

Look for cattle that appear to be healthy and controllable. Just as you want to avoid wild cattle, you want to avoid any cattle that appear listless or stupid. You want a calf that has bright eyes, and in fact has two good eyes. Occasionally, a calf with a sight problem in one eye may have been overlooked in the initial sort. If he can't see, he'll run into you. Once in a while you'll get into some cattle that have some pinkeye problems (common to Herefords and English-cross cattle). If you see a calf with an eye that is literally pink and mattered, try to avoid him, as well as other cattle with any other eye problems.

The more you study cattle the easier it is to just look at one and size him up. It comes with time. Again, there are good cutters and people there who know cattle, and they'll help anyone who asks their advice. Before you ride in to compete, get with some of the pros and ask their opinions: "Which one of those calves looks good to you? What do you think I should try to cut? Should I cut shape or try to cut an individual? Do you see any I should avoid?"

You'll win more money cutting gentle cattle, and not making mistakes, than you will on wild cattle. The wilder cattle will certainly present more of a challenge to your horse, but at the same time they'll create the opportunity for you or the horse to make more mistakes.

If you're low on the list to cut, watch those who cut ahead of you. Try to avoid cattle you notice have already been lost or appeared hard to control. As I said, it's easier for beginners to pick cattle they don't want to cut, rather than to pick an individual they do want. With experience, however, they'll end up cutting individuals more and more, especially in mixed herds.

7 SHOWING AND WINNING

Adequate
preparation and a
positive attitude
are the keys
to success.

Consistency is the key to winning in this sport. A person develops consistency if he is willing to keep an open mind, if he is honest with himself and with his horse, and above all, if he maintains a positive attitude. It doesn't matter whether a person has a great horse, or whether he is a born competitor or a natural rider. If he enters that arena harboring negative thoughts, he is placing himself at a disadvantage before he even begins to work.

Perhaps it's partly a sign of nervousness on the part of some people that you hear talking about negative things, but don't let yourself get caught up in it. You'll naturally visit with other folks at a cutting contest; cutting is a very social activity. But when someone starts talking about how bad the cattle are, or how hard the ground is, or how bad the judge is, I just tune out of the conversation. If a person thinks ahead of time that he's going to lose a cow because the cattle are a little wild, he'll probably lose a cow.

When I spot someone I know who has a problem with his attitude, and he comes up and just casually asks how I am, I'll answer him like this. I'll say, "Why I'm doing just great! Couldn't be any better. How are you?" It just shocks 'em. And pretty soon, I may see this same person coming around to visit more often, and I'll notice he isn't talking about all the things that might go wrong.

I think a person needs to work on himself mentally, and needs to work on his own riding and showing skills, more than he needs to work on training or correcting his horse. Just figure you're going to show your horse to the best of your ability; you're going to cut clean and quit clean, and you'll probably get in there and do a very good job.

Preparation

Preparation also plays a part in being consistent, and goes hand in hand with a positive, winning attitude. A person needs to spend time practicing and training with his horse. And he needs to take plenty of time warming up at a cutting. Don't just rush in there and lope four or five circles, and then try to cut. Arrive early enough to long-trot and gallop your horse, so he is warmed up properly. How long does it take to warm up your horse? Fifteen minutes? Thirty minutes? Longer? You'll know after working with that horse at home. Remember, too, that maybe when he gets to town, he'll have a little more anxiety to work off, and it may take longer to warm him up.

Take a look at the arena. If the cattle are coming in and going out of a center gate, and they're being settled right in front of that gate, it won't matter which way you enter the herd. But if the cattle have been in and out of the arena a time or two, and they're entering through one gate and exiting through another, that will tell you something. If you enter the herd near the out-gate to push cattle up the middle of the arena, they'll naturally flow back around you faster than they will if you enter the herd from the opposite side. You'll start your push toward the out-gate, then turn and push up the middle, and they won't be in quite as much of a hurry to get back to the herd, because they're watching that exit to see if it opens. As a result, you'll have more time to shape up the cow you want to cut.

You can go into the herd for a cut from either side. Most people seem to want to make their first cut from the right—that is, turning left—into the herd. It probably has to do with having their left hand on the reins—it's a little easier to turn left—but you can cut from either side. And a lot of times it depends on your horse; if for some reason the horse is not real comfortable coming in from one particular side, you might try the other.

Look at the ground. Is it hard or soft? If it's hard, the horse will probably have a different feel to him. He probably won't stop as hard, because there's going to be more shock on his feet. He may feel bouncy. So don't let something like that surprise you. You'll probably also have to be less aggressive with him, riding him across the arena. Don't try to really urge him to run and head cattle, because he'll already be on faster dirt; just let him stay parallel with cattle, so he's not trailing. He might also be more aggressive toward cattle, and want to step toward them more on that hard ground. So be ready for that; be prepared to apply some cow-side leg pressure to ride him away from cattle.

On the other hand, if the ground is real deep, real sandy, he's going to get into the ground harder, but you're going to have to ride him out of the turns in a stronger fashion. He'll feel pretty good. If it's real heavy ground, and it's a hot day, he's going to run out of air faster than normal. So, when you ride in to compete, think, "I'm going to take a little more time in my cut. I'm going to go deeper into the cattle, and drive a bunch of them out, and I'll have my help do what they can to give me more time when I'm making my cut." There won't be as much time spent actually working a cow, but it will be more valuable time, because the horse will be sharper. After the first cow has been cut and worked, turn around and take some more time with the next cut; let the horse catch his breath. Whether you wind up cutting two cows or three, take some time. You never want to appear as though you're killing time, of course. It all comes down

to getting 100 percent out of the horse on that day under those conditions.

Before I start to cut on a horse on a hot day like that, I sure wouldn't have loped him around to the point where he was out of air. I would have warmed him up pretty good, and then made sure he had ample time to catch his breath and was comfortable when we were ready to compete. Considering things like this often is the difference between winning and losing, and it all ties in with consistency.

Make sure the equipment is adjusted properly and is neat. The straps on the bridle should be tucked into the keepers. Make sure the tail on the back cinch is in the keeper. A back cinch is optional; it will keep the back of the saddle from popping up and down, but some horses are somewhat "goosey" about working with one. But if I have a back cinch, I don't want it hanging down with five or

Cutting horses require good grooming, the same as other show-type horses. This means clipping a bridle path, clipping away long facial hair, and closely clipping the ears and lower legs, especially around fetlocks and coronet bands. Lance holds his mare while I work on the bridle path.

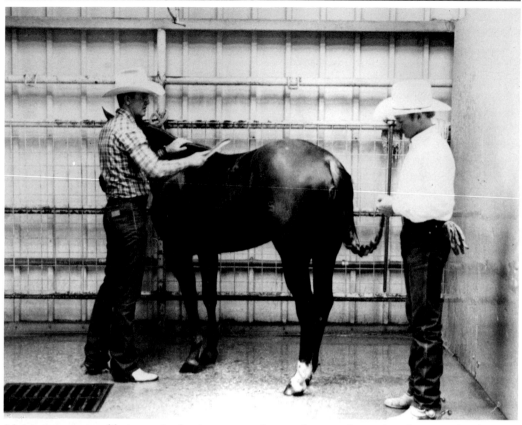

Maintaining a good haircoat is also important; horses that are shown in winter need to be blanketed in cool climates in order to keep their summertime haircoats. I also like to give a horse a bath after a workout. I'm scraping the water off this mare, while Dale Parker unbraids the tail. We braid up tails before a training session to protect them; sometimes a horse with a long tail will step on it and break off hairs when he's stopping and turning, if the tail isn't braided up.

six inches of slack under the horse's belly. I train with a variety of saddles, but I get out my favorite saddle to show in. I also use a nice saddle blanket I keep strictly for showing.

As mentioned previously, you want to evaluate the cattle, check the horse's feet to make sure they're clean, and recheck the cinch, to make sure it's tight. Finally, adjust your reins to make certain they're where you want them when you lower your hand to begin work.

When making a cut, if I see a cow I want that's shaping up pretty good, standing still, looking at me, and the other cattle are moving out of the way, I might take a step toward that cow—not a run, but one step—to further separate her from the others. If she's already moving, and I still want her, I might back up a couple steps to maintain the distance I want, and then move laterally with her. If the cattle are trying to flow back around you in a hurry and you need more time, step into that flow to stop them, then go ahead and cut a spe-

cific cow. If the cattle are wild, a beginner is better off to not cut a specific cow, especially if she's near you on one side, and there are still several cows moving from farther out on your other side; it'll be hard to hold her up and have a smooth cut with cattle going every direction. In that situation, you're smarter to let that cow go, if you haven't declared yourself, and then cut something that will give you the advantage.

But if it's a cow you really want, and it's worth it to you, you may have to do a lot of reining to shape her up, and you might receive a penalty point, too, for not dropping your hand soon enough. And your horse may be a little apprehensive about the cow. It won't look smooth. I think the smoother and more confident you appear, the better it will look to the judge, and the more positive he'll be about the marking.

The distance you're going to work away from the herd will vary. On wild cattle, you'll want to start farther away, because a wild cow will put more pressure on your horse trying to get back to the herd, and it will help the horse to have room to back away from that cow, to give her ground during the work. You'll also start farther away from the herd so you don't disturb the cattle and get a penalty for picking up cattle.

For a horse that tends to be chargey, aggressive, and moves toward cattle, it's best to start him closer to the herd, because he'll want to move toward the cow anyway. Some horses are more comfortable working close to a herd; for others, it doesn't seem to make any difference. This distance from the herd will depend on the cattle, how wild they are, what chance you have of disturbing them, and how your horse likes to work and you like to present him.

When you quit a cow, be as smooth as you possibly can. Make sure the cow is either standing still, or is moving away from you, to avoid the penalty for a hot quit. Look confident, run that quick mental check on yourself, and if you think you're getting up, relax. Then smooth out your reins and quietly enter the herd for another cut.

No matter how your run is going, don't allow yourself to look discouraged. Or if you do something you're not sure about, don't look around for someone else, as though you're asking "Did I do wrong?" Never let 'em know you think something was wrong. A lot of times it doesn't look as bad as it feels. I'm not talking about doing something flagrant, like losing a cow, but the little things, like maybe the horse isn't stopping the way you'd like him to, or maybe he loses his working advantage at one point. If you shake your head and look disgusted, the judge will naturally think, "Well, he's not liking it, so I'm not liking it."

When that whistle blows, or the buzzer sounds, and you quit, and you look like you loved every second of it, chances are that even if there was a minor mistake in there, that judge will go ahead and mark you well. If a person can learn to show a horse with a lot of poise and confidence, he'll be consistent and win a lot of prizes.

Years ago I had a horse named Nu Bar that I loved to show. He was a hard-stopping horse and a lot of fun to ride, and I showed him one day under an old judge at the Sun Circuit in Arizona. This horse wasn't on 100 percent that day; he was giving me about 75 percent, and that was killing me, because he just wasn't stopping as hard or as crisp as he could. I don't know if it was the weather, or just him, or if I was riding him too strong, or what. But a little over two minutes into the run, I decided I couldn't stand it anymore. When we went over to one of the sides, I just stuck him in the ground. Just stopped and backed, and made him turn over his hocks, and ran and stopped again. Then I turned him loose and he really tried. They blew the whistle and I rode out, and in those days you had to automatically ride up to the judge and take off the bridle so he could look at the bit (whereas today you ride past the judge and he tells you if he wants a closer look at your headgear). So when I got off, that judge said to me, "Son, I don't understand you, takin' ahold of that horse like that and stopping. You were gonna win the cutting."

I'd given away a 45-horse cutting, just because the horse wasn't working up to my satisfaction. If I'd gone ahead and ridden him for that last 30 seconds, I would have won. That taught me a valuable lesson. What I should have done was waited until later to work a cow with him, if I still felt he needed it. I should have run a check on myself, evaluated the way I was riding him, considered the type of cattle we were cutting, given the run some serious thought.

Horse Care on the Road

Through the years, I have found that the better I take care of a horse I'm hauling to cuttings, the better that horse will work. I keep close tabs on his physical condition, checking his back and legs for any signs of soreness; periodically, I'll have a veterinarian check his teeth and do a blood count on him. I watch the diet, and believe in feeding vitamin and mineral supplements. When I start out on the road, I'll haul as much of the feed he is used to as I can, and if I see where I'm going to run out of feed and have to buy hay or grain that's different, I'll make the switch gradually.

I wrap legs for hauling, to give them extra support, and to protect them from injury. I use a leg bracer before I wrap,

We're ready to load up and head out for a cutting.

Albert Templeton shows how I like to wrap legs before hauling. A leg bracer, like Absorbine, is first applied, then comes a soft cotton pad (left) which is kept in place by a wrap (right) that is applied slightly snug, but not tight.

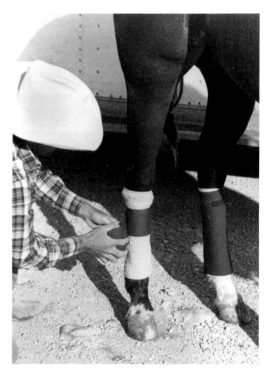

and everyone has their own way of doing this. You can use straight rubbing alcohol or alcohol and glycerin; Absorbine is the greatest old standby in the world. But if you don't use anything, you should still wrap their legs. I also keep a lot of shavings in the bottom of the trailer—at least six inches on top of the rubber pad. And if I'm doing a lot of hauling, I'll have an extra rubber pad on the floor, in other words, two pads, for more cushion and to cut down on the road heat coming up through the floor.

When I'm hauling, I also make sure I unload a horse at least every six to eight hours. I'll walk him around, offer him some water. When I arrive at my destination, I'll walk him around some more before putting him in a stall. Next morning, I'll check on how much water he drank, how much he ate. For a horse that won't drink on the road, I like to put a little Karo syrup in his water each day for several days before we leave, and then continue to add the syrup. Water from different locations will still taste "like home" to him.

If a horse seems to be backing off in training, or not showing up to his ability, that's the time to run a good check

44

on him, to see if something is wrong. A horse has to want to work for you. It's very hard to just "make" a horse work if he doesn't want to. You'll end up working him longer, harder, being stronger with him; and that will just add to the problem. It'll be a losing proposition.

You also want your horse to look his best, to be clipped up and groomed, and have a nice haircoat just like any other show horse. A real long-haired horse won't look as good as a horse that has been blanketed in winter, brushed, and kept up properly. A little corn oil in the grain (perhaps ½ cup daily) is great for haircoats.

At home or on the road, I give a horse a bath after he has been ridden, unless the weather is cold. A good way to keep manes and tails in good shape is to apply hair conditioner to them when they are wet. Don't brush. Just let them dry, and they'll be free of tangles. Manes and tails are brushed sparingly, only when they are dry, to avoid pulling out hair.

Consult with your vet. Establish a regular vaccination and worming program. I like to worm four times a year, alternating between paste and tube worming. It's also a good idea to have your vet help you put together a good medicine chest for home and for the road. Get some things for possible emergencies and learn how to use them.

When it comes to a horse's health, inside and out, you can't give him too much care. A horse that shows good care is just another sign that you're professional. And that's what we're trying to accomplish throughout—to present a professional competent look to that judge, whether you're a beginner, non-pro, or full-time professional trainer and cutter.

Attitude

One thing a person needs to realize: If he isn't winning, and if he does have a good horse, then there's probably only one thing wrong. He needs to make some changes in himself. That's the bad news. The good news is, a person can change. As soon as he quits blaming his help, blaming the horse, or blaming the judges, the realization will come: "I've got to get better. I'm not going to get trickier, I'm going to improve." And that

will take some self-discipline. And it will probably require some listening. I've seen people who came to a cutting clinic for help. I'll tell them something; they'll tell me something. Pretty soon I can't figure out who's teaching whom. Those people aren't going to win until they learn to have an open mind and learn to listen.

I learned a valuable lesson along these lines many years ago when I was working for G.D. Turnbow, on the horse division of one of his ranches in California. He was an elderly man at the time, but very energetic, and acted like a much younger man. Mr. Turnbow also had the reputation for being a hard man to work for, and when I went to work for him, some folks said I wouldn't be there 60 days. I wound up working for him for seven years, and it was quite an education for me.

One day Mr. Turnbow came out to the ranch and said, "Leon, you know I'd like to see your list of reasons for not doing as well as you should be doing. I know you have the ability, but I don't feel you're doing as well as you should, so I'd like to see your list of reasons for not doing well."

Caught off guard, I told him I didn't have my list with me. So he said, "Well, tonight when you come over to the house to go over the horse program, bring your list of reasons for not doing good."

I went home for lunch at noon and started preparing my list. I put down everything I could think of, blaming some of the people I worked with, some of the horses I was training. I blamed my car, for not running very good; I think I even blamed the neighbors for not loaning me any money, and to heck with 'em. You know, I gave this list a lot of thought.

So, that night when I went over to Mr. Turnbow's house, I took my list of reasons for not doing good, and presented it to him. He looked over my list carefully, and when he got through it, he looked at me and said, "Leon, this is a pretty impressive list, and the only thing wrong with it is you left off something."

"What's that?" I asked.

He said, "You're not on it."

Well, he proceeded to convince me that I should tear up my list of reasons

45

Naturally, I'm pleased that my son, Lance (in the photo at right), is doing well in cutting. In the above photo, that's me on Smart Date at Memphis. These two pictures are displayed together on a wall in my office. **Photo by Pat Hall**

for not doing good, and come up with a new list, and the only name on that new list should be mine. His point was well taken—if I worked on myself to get better and to accomplish what I wanted to do, and quit blaming other sources, my life would pick up greatly, financially and professionally. From that day on, the only one on that list has been myself.

Mr. Turnbow was a grand old man, and I loved for him to come to the ranch. Everyone else, it seemed, was kind of nervous about his visits. You could see last-minute preparations. He had several ranches, but this particular ranch I

worked on was about 20,000 acres in the San Joaquin Valley, and the day they got wind that he'd be coming, you'd see everyone rushing around trying to get things shaped up. He loved perfection.

I made it a point on the horse division to keep things up at all times, so if he drove in at 2 or 3 o'clock in the morning, which he was capable of doing, I didn't have to worry about it. I could be happy to see him and not be worried about what was going on at the ranch.

He told me one time he wanted me to accomplish the impossible in my life. He said if you try to accomplish the impos-

46

Photo by Pat Hall

sible, you probably will, and one thing you won't have to worry about is competition, because there will probably be very little competition. It's people like him who have influenced me and been greatly responsible for the success I've enjoyed.

Once you get the basic knowledge involved with cutting and showing, then it comes down to attitude and the goals you've set for yourself. Maybe your goal is to win the $2,000 non-pro, or to be a world champion. Or maybe the goal is to play at cutting, but to be as tough as you can be on that weekend. Have fun

with cutting, whatever your goal is. You don't have to like it when you lose, but just tell yourself you'll be tougher tomorrow. You'll go through slumps—everyone does—but there's nothing better than overcoming one of them. When you get in one of those slumps, and just can't seem to win anything, just figure there's only one way, and that's up. They can't keep you from winning if you've got the right attitude. Prepare yourself and your horse. A winner will always find a way to win.

8 TRAINING

Philosophy

The philosophy in training a horse to cut is the same as teaching a person to cut. I want to show both how easy it is, not how hard it is. There's no trunk of tricks connected with any of this. Horse training is just good, basic logic: teaching the horse to run, stop, and turn around in order to control a cow. He learns to press up to a cow, and to press off a cow. If I ask a horse to hold his position in the arena while working, he holds it. I want to teach him to not be aggressive toward cattle, which is a reversal of his natural inclination. I want to teach him to listen to me through my cues, and to understand that I can help him in cutting a cow out of the herd, and help him get to the right positions, to take some pressure away so he is able to control a cow with the least amount of effort. I want to build trust in the horse; I want him to understand that I'm not going to confuse or hurt him, or let him get into a situation where he can hurt himself. I want to build up the horse's confidence in himself and his ability to control a cow.

One of the aspects of horse training that keeps it interesting for me is that no two horses train exactly alike. I've gradually come to realize that there's no limit to what I can learn as a trainer. Every time I think I've got it all figured out, a new strain of colts will come along and either move or think differently than the last ones, and I'll have to try to adapt to them in some of their ways. I want to meet the horse at least halfway in training. I want to figure him out, strike up a

partnership with him. Maybe he won't do something quite the way I'd prefer, but I want to be open-minded enough to be willing to adapt to him, to create that harmony between us.

At some point in training, a person also must evaluate whether the horse is going to be a star, whether he is going to be average, or whether he is going to not do much in cutting. Some horses just don't have the mind for it. They may do fine when you're working them and helping them to cut—to turn and run and stop. But they may show you they're not willing to go on and take the responsibility for controlling a cow on their own, when you're not picking up the reins and giving them definite cues or direction with a cow. They don't always go ahead and fulfill your expectations. But if a horse has the desire, he'll let you know, and if he has the athletic ability, that horse will probably turn out to be one you can win on. The average horse is the one that can be discouraging in training. You see he has the ability, but he's just progressing at an average pace, and there are things you wish he would start picking up on, but he isn't. Well, that's the horse you just have to wait on. He'll need more time. The real good horses have a different feel to them; it's almost electrifying to see this brilliance, this alertness and interest in whatever the cow is doing. After I've had a horse in training four or five months, he'll tell me whether he's going to be great at cutting, average, or needs to find another career.

Here's a general description of my training procedures, what I do with

48

young horses that I want to prepare for the NCHA Futurity at the end of their third year. The procedure would be the same for an older horse, keeping in mind that the schedule will vary from horse to horse. One key to success is to keep injuries to a minimum. This is accomplished to a large degree by keeping a horse well-conditioned, and by always warming him up properly before a training session.

The Schedule

With an eye toward the Futurity, ideally I like to get colts and fillies started—on cattle, if possible—by June of their second year. They can begin a light training program and be working a cow pretty good by the time they are three. Before I put a horse on cattle, I want to make sure he has learned the basics. I don't want him to be running, sliding, and spinning, I just want him to be able to lope around a circle on the proper lead, and when I pick up the bridle reins he stops and backs on cue, and will be responsive to head direction. He should respond to leg pressure. If a horse can do these basic maneuvers, he's ready to be put on cattle.

I like to work a horse with cattle four days a week, preferably two days in a row, then skip a day, and then work two more days. On his off days, he won't be just standing around in his stall, he'll be ridden outside for an hour or so, just a nice, leisurely ride in the hills, walking and trotting, maybe doing some loping, but nothing hard. This outside riding keeps a horse's mind fresh; he won't sour on the arena work. If a person doesn't have access to riding anywhere other than in an arena, he can still keep the horse fresh by using those off days for a leisurely ride in the arena, with no cattle involved and no pressure. One of those off days might be well spent by just turning the horse loose in the arena or prefer-

ably a paddock or pasture.

If working cattle two days in a row seems like it's too much for a colt, I might try working him every other day for a while. If he just isn't progressing with cow work, I might try working him with cattle three days in a row, and then riding him outside two days in a row. As training continues, I evaluate a colt and try to figure out what schedule is best for him.

Something else we do with a lot of colts is take them for a ride outside before we begin the arena work. This works very well for a colt that is high-strung, hyper. After the ride, I'll bring him to the arena or round pen, lope a few circles, and his mind will be fresh and he won't be quite so apprehensive. We'll work a few cows on him and put him up. This saves time and cattle, and also keeps his mistakes to a minimum.

Before he goes to the stall, he'll be cooled out and given a bath. And that night, before I go to the house, I'll look at him and make sure he appears healthy and comfortable. A schedule like this is geared to avoid constantly pressuring a horse. Horses must have time to think, time to rest; when I'm riding one, I don't ride him until he's exhausted. When he is working up to what I think is his potential, when he shows signs of grasping a particular move we've been working on, that's the time to stop. It would be a mistake to cut some more cows, trying to get him to do that particularly nice move again and again, because that situation might not materialize for a while, and he'll end up tired and get to the point where he doesn't care whether he does something right or wrong. It becomes drudgery to him and he'll begin to lose ground in his training. Let the horse work and *study* a cow as much as possible. Remember: A person who "dinks" with his horse all the time winds up with a "dink" for a horse.

One of the keys to making a good horse is repetition. The work will be pretty much the same for the first six to nine months—hunt that cow, stop, turn.

Snaffle bit with running martingale. Note the adjustment of the running martingale (above). I can hold up the ring on each rein, and it will nearly touch the middle of the horse's neck.

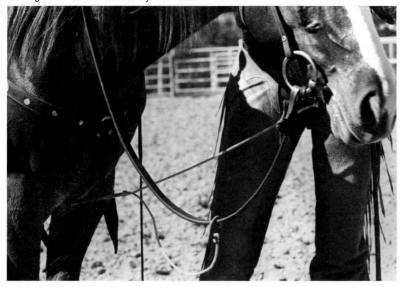

Headgear

I get the best results out of a snaffle bit and running martingale, and an Argentine bit and martingale, that first year in training. I'll evaluate a colt when he comes in—lope him around, stop, back. If he's pretty green and isn't responding properly to the snaffle, I'll put him in a pen and check him around to the right for 15 minutes, to the left for 15 minutes, and straight back for 15 minutes, to start developing some feel and control in him. If a horse has perhaps been injured in his mouth or is really head-shy about a bit, then I'll go to a bosal. I'll ride him outside and in the arena, and just work to get him responsive to the bosal. A lot of people use bosals on all the horses they start, and there's nothing wrong with that. I prefer to use a snaffle whenever possible.

We'll go along with a snaffle bit, or Argentine bit, and martingale for the rest of that year, and then use this combination at least off and on during the three-year-old year. Sometimes, on older horses, I'll still go back to this if we need to work on basics. If I know I'll be doing a lot of handling with the reins, a lot of head positioning, or a lot of backing, I'll use the snaffle.

When I take a colt out of a regular snaffle and start trying to develop more feel in his mouth, I may go to a twisted-wire snaffle, and then to a bit that still has a broken mouthpiece—something with short, loose shanks on it, like the Argentine. This progression is for horses that are starting to understand the game; they're stopping with a cow, turning with a cow, learning to control a cow. With the Argentine, I can begin applying a little pressure under the chin, so the horse learns to stop from that pressure as well as the pull on the mouth. Also, with this type of bit, you can get a lot of head direction; you can use two hands on the

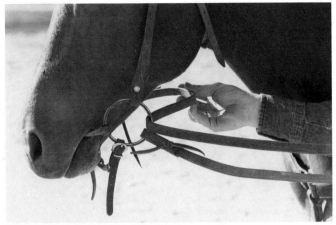

This is how I like to check up a horse to one side. 1/ Running the rein from the opposite side through the ring on the snaffle will prevent the snaffle bit from being pulled through the horse's mouth when his head is tied around.

2/ The reins are then brought through the back dee ring on the saddle. The fellow checking this horse around is Dale Parker.

3/ The horse's head is gently pulled to the side.

4/ Then the reins are tied off at the saddle horn.

The horse is left alone, but observed, in a safe pen for about 15 minutes. He'll learn to give his head to relieve the pressure of a direct pull. The same procedure will be used to check him around on the other side.

To check a horse straight back, the rein on each side is brought through the back dee ring and then tied at the horn.

Here's the best way to hold your reins while working with a horse in training, when you know you'll be alternately riding with two hands for direct reining, and with one hand on the reins to see if the horse has learned what you've been trying to teach him. We call this the cutter's cross; the right rein (top) can be pushed easily through the left hand, and the right hand can go to the horn (below). This enables the rider to concentrate on his posture, helping the horse through strong moves. It's easy to pull the right rein out again for direct reining.

1/

2/

3/

4/

This shows how to form the cutter's cross. 1/ Index finger on the left hand splits the reins. 2/ The left rein passes over the middle finger. 3/ The tails of both reins hang on the left side, and the right hand holds the right rein. 4/ The reins are bridged.

reins and tip a horse's head to really get him to look at a cow, and it also reinforces that stop without scaring him. This type of bit also gets him used to packing more weight in his mouth.

At some point in his three-year-old year, I'll make a gradual transition to some type of grazing bit, like a Buster Welch, something with a low port. I want to stay away from long-shanked bits altogether, as long as I can maintain the control with a mild bit. The key is to find that grazing bit that provides the control and response, and upsets him the least when he's working with it. I'll use that same bit for a lot of outside riding, so he becomes comfortable with it. Copper on a bit is up to the trainer and the horse. You might have a horse that likes it. If you're still having problems in getting the response and control you want on a horse, then try some other bits, and make sure you learn how those bits are supposed to be adjusted, and how they're supposed to work on a horse. Any bit is only as good as the hands using it. The key to success with a bit is in the application.

It's fine to use the racehorse cross for direct reining if you're certain you'll have two hands on the reins throughout a training session. This would be strictly for slow work. Note that the tail of each rein hangs on the opposite side; it's difficult to go to one hand on the reins with this cross.

When you stop a horse with the reins a little high, a little wide, you start stopping a horse with your biceps. You're using a lot of power. You can do the same thing with your hands down low, with arms extended, stopping a horse with your finger tips and forearms.

Avoid holding the reins up high, like this.

This is a two-year-old mare that we're ready to put on cattle for the first time. To warm up, I've loped a few circles in both directions in the round pen, and now I'm working on some flexing exercises. I ask the horse to turn her head toward me, first to one side, then the other.

Now we're walking in circles, flexing while moving. Notice the light touch on the reins. While flexing the horse's head to the left with my hands, I'm also applying some inside leg pressure. By doing this, in both directions, the horse learns to respond to leg pressure so I can ride away from a cow if necessary, and also get the head turned for good eye contact with that cow.

To clarify: "Inside leg" means the leg to the inside of an arc or circle; it also means the leg between horse and cow that is being worked. "Outside leg" means the opposite— the leg on the outside of the horse's arc or circle, or the leg between horse and herd.

Another variation in flexing exercises: I'm moving in a circle, asking the horse to flex to the outside, while also using outside leg pressure. The legs cross over one another, in front and back.

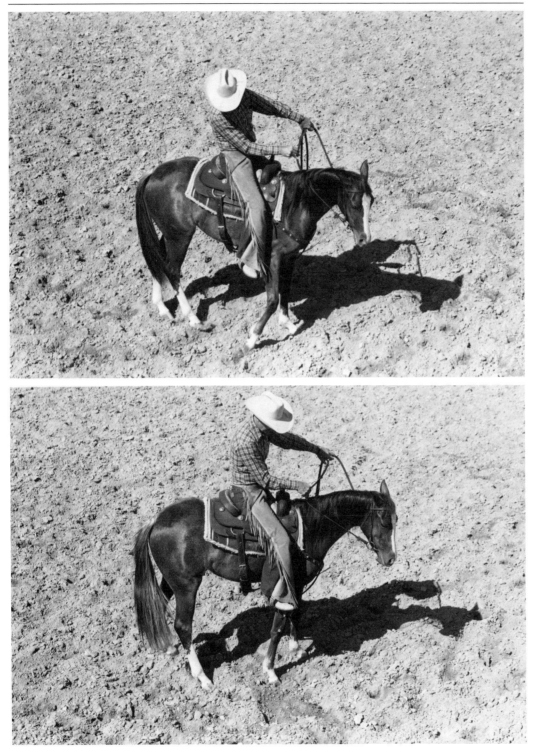

More work on moving the horse's rib cage. I'm using inside leg pressure while flexing the horse's head to the right. Teaching a horse to move away from leg pressure, and to turn his head like this during the dry work (work without a cow in the pen) will be useful later on. This is the same procedure we'll use on a horse that is traveling parallel with a cow but trying to move into the cow. I can press that rib cage away from the cow and at the same time tip the horse's head toward the cow for plenty of eye contact. This teaches the horse to watch what the cow is doing.

Starting on Cattle

When I put a horse on cattle—day one—I'll first lope him around so he isn't too fresh, just warmed up and relaxed, and then we'll go to the large round pen. I'll put one gentle cow in there, nothing at all wild acting, and just ride the horse to the cow and kind of follow the cow around. I want the horse to simply realize there's something in there besides him.

I'll watch the horse's reactions, to see what type of horse he is. In their initial reactions to cattle, one horse will be afraid of the cow, another will not even acknowledge a cow, and another will want to lay back his ears and bite at the cow. But regardless of the first response, I'll get the horse to just move this cow around, walking and trotting. When the cow stops, I'll stop the horse. We'll do this for maybe 20 minutes or so the first couple of days. The horse may not even break a sweat—I don't want to get him too tired. By the end of that second session, I hope to have reassured the timid horse that the cow is nothing to be afraid of; I want the disinterested horse to have discovered that it is more interesting to look at the cow and follow her around than it is to ignore her; I want the aggressive horse to know that I'll pull him up, and won't let him be overly aggressive to the cow.

When we come back to the round pen after those two sessions, and the cow has been turned in, we'll step toward her and I'll have both hands on the reins, for direct reining. When the cow moves, I'll direct the horse to move off parallel to her, rather than follow her from behind. If the cow walks, we walk; if the cow trots, we trot. If the cow runs off, we won't run after her, we'll just trot over there to her, and keep everything slow and easy for the horse. When the cow stops, I'll stop the horse and just sit there and make sure he has good eye contact with the cow. If I need to tip his head toward the cow a bit to maintain eye contact, I can do it. My hands will be low and I'll pull on the inside rein enough to turn his head slightly toward the cow. We'll sit there for several seconds, then step toward the cow again. When the cow moves, it's the same pro-

Day one: The mare and I are in the round pen (which has a diameter of 145 feet), and a single cow has just been turned into the pen with us. What follows next will be pretty much the standard routine for training over the next 30 days. There will be a lot of walking and trotting around the pen with one cow, and I'll make sure the horse is always looking at that cow, whether we're moving or standing still. There will be no hard moves—look at the slack in the reins as we approach the cow, which is moving around the pen.

My hands are down, the horse is relaxed. There's some slack in the reins, but I have them gathered enough so I can give the horse head direction to maintain eye contact with the cow when necessary.

The cow wants to move off at a pretty good pace, but we're in no hurry to catch up.

This shows excellent eye contact. I've used my hands to make sure the horse is watching the cow. Below: Remember the flexing exercises? I've got the mare's head turned toward the cow, and I'm using inside leg pressure (my left leg) to flex her rib cage away from the cow.

cedure; we'll move parallel to her at a walk or trot. In the next day or two, we may lope periodically to stay parallel with the cow. The cow will travel in complete circles around the pen, and she'll also stop and turn. When she turns, we'll turn with her.

I start helping the colt turn by using some leg pressure. If I'm turning to the right, I'll use my left leg against him, and vice-versa. I'll always give him that head direction first; I'll turn his head in the direction the cow is turning, then follow it up with outside leg pressure while making the turn. I also can use leg pressure to keep his body straight for a stop. If he's moving across the pen and his body is bent, traveling crooked (which isn't unusual for a young horse at this stage of his training), I can apply leg pressure to straighten him up. It's essential that a horse stops straight; if his rib cage is bent to the right, and he needs to make a right-hand turn, he'll have to reposition all that bone structure in or-

1/ Here's a sequence that shows the cow moving away from the fence and cutting across the round pen at a trot, and then a lope. We follow along at a leisurely pace, watching her all the time, and regain control on the other side. This is basically all we do the first month—stop, turn, maintain eye contact.

2/

3/

4/

der to turn, and then he might start elevating his shoulder in a turn. You want to develop a turn, ultimately, that is similar to a rollback, in that the horse turns over his hocks, but his head and shoulder need to stay low so he can maintain good eye contact with the cow, and so he has a low center of gravity, enabling him to get into the ground again very quickly and not be out-maneuvered.

Colts that aren't responding well to leg pressure may need to have that pressure reinforced with a spur occasionally. It helps if the horse has been shown what response is expected when he feels a spur, before he's in a pen, concentrating on a cow. If he doesn't move away from leg pressure, touch him with a spur. I like to use the spur as a prod, to just touch him with it on the side. I never rear back and jab a horse with a spur; that will just make him tense. Later on in his training, if he seems a little lazy about getting his front end around in a turn, I might use an outside spur on his shoulder. Again, the spur shouldn't be used to abuse a horse, but rather to get his attention when he isn't responding to

5/

6/

61

Helping the horse through turns (above and below), with leg and rein cues. The mare maintains good eye contact, we make the turns, but there are no hard moves involved.

leg pressure the way you want him to.

At this stage of training, I'm not trying to make the colt really hustle through the moves or do anything hard. I'm just teaching him to run, stop with cattle, and when a cow turns, he turns. I'll continue to use slow, gentle cattle, still one on one, without a herd of cattle in the pen.

Some colts take to cutting right away. I may feel a colt want to stop on his own and turn with a cow the first day we start working like this. Usually, though, it takes a few days of this type of work, and by then most horses will begin stopping on their own. I'll continue to position the head for eye contact. I want to try to hold a horse's concentration on a cow as long as possible. A horse that is

1/ Here's another series, still day one, that shows me helping this mare through her turns.

concentrating on the cow will learn to outsmart her, and that's preferable to having a wild athlete that seeks only to out-maneuver one. The good cutting horses literally learn to read cattle. They control a cow by watching and thinking, as well as reacting.

The horse's natural tendency in the beginning, generally speaking, is to want to drive cattle, to move them off. This tendency needs to be reversed; the horse should learn to approach a cow with caution in order to control her. I won't let a horse take a run at a cow. When we approach a cow, we'll take our time, a step at a time. If a horse wants to move toward her while we're traveling parallel to her, I'll use leg pressure to move him away. Work on taking away this natural drover tendency in the horse at this stage will help prevent him from becoming aggressive later on.

2/

3/

4/

5/

6/

This is another two-year-old mare, and she's into her second month of training. We're riding to a cow, I've picked up the reins (below), and I'm helping the mare move off with the cow.

By the start of the second month, a colt should be to the point where, when I start riding to a cow, he isn't trying to just trot right up there; he's showing some caution in getting to her. He's running and stopping with a cow pretty good. When a cow turns around, he turns around on his own; he's not trying to beat the cow out of that turn, but should be just turning with her and flowing with the movements. From this point on, most moves he makes will start to get stronger. I'll encourage him to travel faster, to stay up with a cow, and to stop harder. He should be turning over his hocks pretty well and gaining confidence. And all the time I'm keeping this thing just as simple as possible. No pressure. I'm there to help him with any maneuver.

At this point, I don't begin to make a horse pick up his front end and really crack back over his hocks in a turn. I won't reach up and spur him in the shoulder. Instead, I'm going to spend some time working on a maneuver that involves anticipating when the cow is going to turn. This is the only time you literally anticipate something involved with cutting. We'll be working quietly, at a walk or trot, and I won't let the horse get long on the cow. I won't let him get his head past the cow's head to turn her.

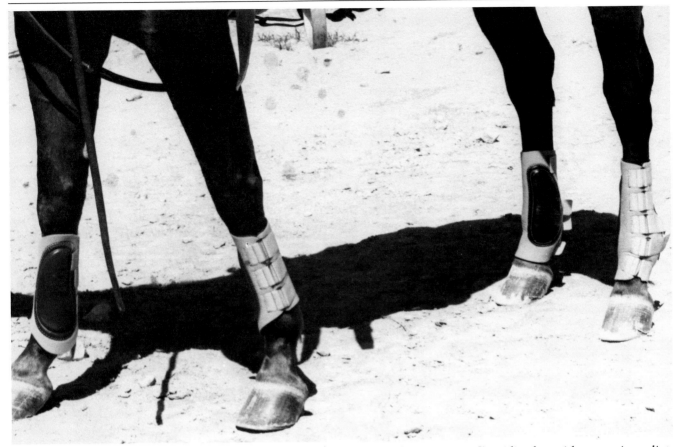

This mare is trying to do a few more things; her moves are getting a little stronger, so I'm riding her with protective splint boots on the front legs, and combination boots (splint and skid boots) on the hind legs.

We'll stay short on the cow, and follow her to the side of the pen. She'll stop, turn, and move off. If she moves off down the pen a little ways before actually turning back to the side, that's fine. But instead of allowing the horse to turn with her, we'll back up a few steps, maintain good eye contact, stay parallel with the cow a few steps, then wait for a couple seconds as the cow moves off. Then when I do let the horse turn, he really wants to turn. His hindquarters will be under him, because of the backing, and when he turns he'll come around pretty strong over those hocks. This maneuver teaches a horse to read a cow; on down the road, he'll be pretty hard to trick, because of this practice. This also builds up his confidence; he learns that even if he is out of working position temporarily, he can catch up to the cow and continue working her. I don't want him to come out of the turn so strong that he gets long on a cow (out in front of her). I want him to learn to just flow with the cow, always maintaining eye contact, synchronizing with the cow in stops and turns.

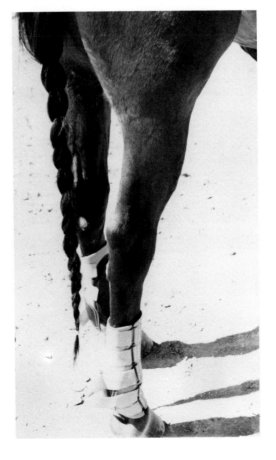

To protect tails, to keep them looking good for the show ring, we'll usually braid them like this before a training or riding session. When a horse is working, getting into the ground and staying low while controlling a cow, a long flowing tail can be stepped on, and some of the hairs can be broken or pulled out. This is a simple three-strand braid, held at the end with a rubberband.

1/ Here's the backing exercise I use to develop style in a horse's turns. We were at a walk or trot, and were short on the cow. The cow has turned, but instead of letting the horse turn, we begin backing, staying parallel with the cow.

2/

3/

4/ After backing four, five, or six steps, I let the horse turn.

5/

6/And we re-gain our position on the cow, moving in the opposite direction.

1/ We begin this sequence by noting the good eye contact this mare has with the cow. I've turned her head in just a bit.

2/ We turn with the cow.

3/ The mare follows through the turn nicely.

4/ *And notice our position on that cow. We're not trying to run up there and head the cow; instead, we're staying a little short on the cow, back by the hip.*

5/ *It's easy for the horse to maintain advantage with a cow on the fence in the round pen. The horse doesn't have to travel as far or as fast as the cow in order to keep up.*

6/ Cow slows down; we slow down.

7/ Cow moves off again and the mare is with her.

8/ Now the cow turns with some intensity, which is reflected in the mare's reaction, and we wind up moving along the fence again in the opposite direction.

9/ The significance of this picture is the fact that the mare has just been through a couple of pretty strong turns—and she's not excited about it! The action has slowed down and she's back to eye contact with the cow. The mare is relaxed, and she is watching.

1/ It's easy to see how the training is progressing on this mare during her second month, working in the round pen, one-on-one with a cow. The moves are getting stronger; we're staying up with the cow.

What I'm doing here is developing a cow horse, and with the backing, I'm beginning to get some style in his turns. He won't elevate his shoulder in a turn like this as long as I keep my hands low, while direct-reining, and give him head direction in a turn. This teaches a horse to stop, wait, look; and when he gets over his hocks in a turn he will "vacuum" that cow from head to tail with total concentration.

I'll continue with this maneuver off and on, perhaps a half-dozen times, during every training session through about the third month. By then the horse should be stopping on his own most of the time, and I'll be very aware of how he stops; his stops should be strong. Throughout this 90 days, I'll spend time

reinforcing a good stop on the hindquarters. I'll do this by stopping the horse on a running cow. When I stop I'll be sitting deep in the saddle, with pockets really under myself, to help him stop.

A horse needs a good stop in the early stages in order to avoid problems later on, in order to avoid stopping on his front end. A horse that gets in the habit of stopping on his front end will make what we call a barrel turn on a cow. When a horse does that, it doesn't necessarily mean he can't hold a cow, but he doesn't have the style to be a top winner. When he does stop, he will have lost all his power behind; he'll have to pull off with his front end, because his hind legs aren't under him to drive out of the turn.

2/ At the same time, I'm showing the mare how to get away from some pressure. We're pressing off from this cow (inside leg pressure) so we don't have to work as hard to keep up. And I'm also giving the mare a little head direction.

3/ We're moving to the other side of the pen.

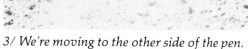

4/ I'm riding with one hand on the reins at this point, allowing the horse to work more on her own, but my right hand is still up, ready to help her with direct reining if she needs it.

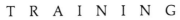

5/

6/

Working one-on-one in the round pen: This goes on frequently throughout training, even for older horses in competition that need to brush up on traveling with a cow and stopping.

7/ I've got two hands on the reins again at this point, because the mare started to get long on the cow, and I wanted to hold her back. I'm teaching her to not only maintain eye contact, and to be able to get away from pressure when necessary, but to also stay on the inside of a cow, to not try to head cattle (get past them).

8/ All I'm doing is showing the horse how simple this work really is.

Some horses with a lot of "cow" in them are going to want to take a step toward a cow that has stopped and hesitated. That's okay, as long as the horse stops straight initially.

Here are a couple of photos showing this same mare in a good turn, working completely on her own. My rein hand is down on her neck, and my right hand is on the saddle horn. She has taken responsibility for controlling the cow.

This horse is about five months along in her training. In the photos that follow, you'll see that her moves are stronger than the previous two horses', that she's working more on her own, and that my training procedures are basically the same. We're working out of the herd, now, which is settled in the middle of the round pen. This horse is in an Argentine bit.

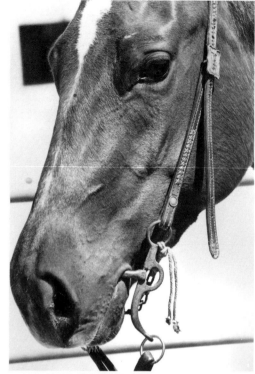

If the colt's training is progressing well by the fourth month, I'll take him out of the snaffle bit, and begin riding him periodically with an Argentine type of bit, something with small shanks, just to get him used to something a little different. This will also get him used to some pressure under the chin with the chin strap. Each time I make a change in bits, I'll begin by checking him up for 15 minutes on each side, and 15 minutes straight back, so he understands the feel of the bit before I ask him to respond to it while we're working. I'll still do a lot of alternating with a snaffle bit and martingale, and if I have any problem with one of the other bits, I'll automatically drop him back to the snaffle or Argentine for a while. I want to use the Argentine bit more and more, but if I encounter a problem with him, to where I want to stop him more, or help him turn faster,

Cattle are brought in (top), moved to the middle of the round pen, and we ride around them until they settle (bottom).

or give him more head direction, I'll use the snaffle and martingale for that training session.

Six Months

After about six months of training, he should be working a cow with a minimum of help from me. But I'll always be prepared to help show him what needs to be done if he needs it. The colt is trying to figure out a few things, and now is the time to begin working him with a herd of cattle. I'll bring in some cattle that have been used and are pretty gentle—maybe 10 or 20 head—and push them to the middle of the round pen. I'll ride around them—walk, trot , lope— until they're settled in the middle. There will probably be one other person horseback in the pen with us, and I'll spend lots of time and patience in getting the horse used to having cattle around him. We'll spend time in the herd, just standing.

Then I'll drive one cow to the fence and go around with her just like I would if it was one-on-one. Pretty soon the cow will get off the fence and try to get back to the herd. We'll stay with her, circling the herd if necessary. The colt will become accustomed to working with that herd near him, and at the same time he is getting more of a challenge from the cow trying to get back to the herd. We'll be moving left and right more than we did before.

If I've cut out a cow that is really eating him up, trying to get back to the herd, I'll try to hold her a few times, but if the cow is putting on pressure and the colt begins to get a little wild or confused, I'll stop. That cow can rejoin the herd and I'll cut out another. If at any

1/ We enter the herd quietly.

2/ And I begin to make my cut.

point the colt acts like he's getting scared and running wild, I'll put him back in the round pen with one cow, work one-on-one for a while, then go back to the herd in the middle. Or if I decide the cattle are just too wild for him, I'll go to real gentle cattle that won't scare him.

The colt will work like this in the round pen and in the arena, periodically, almost until Futurity time, at the end of his three-year-old year. Working cattle in the middle is also a great way to use cattle for a long time and get more out of them. So that's another reason for working with the herd in the middle. And it always gives the advantage to the colt; he can completely circle the herd while working a cow, and won't get trapped in any corners of the arena, trying to control her.

3/ I like this whiteface calf.

4/ I take a step toward her and she begins to move off while the rest of the cattle return to the herd.

5/ I want to take this calf clear to the fence, if possible, to allow plenty of room to work.

6/ The horse approaches in a cautious, and alert, manner.

7/ The calf turns back and we get into some pretty heavy action. The horse shows good concentration, and she is working on her own.

8/

9/

10/

I want to be able
to drive a horse as
far from the herd
as I want, and
have him work
right there.

1/ Here's another view of the same sequence.

2/

3/

4/

You can't force a horse to advance at a certain pace, but if he wants to move along faster than the average horse, then let him.

We're circling the herd on this one, and I've got both hands on the reins, offering a little assistance.

Several times during a training session like this, I'll emphasize the stop. I'll make sure I sit deep in the saddle and take hold of the horse, stopping on a run. Then I'll back a few steps, turn, and resume working.

There's still plenty of slow work for us in each training session, with more backing and turning (top and bottom).

1/ I won't let a cow just "eat up" a horse at this point.

2/ When we cut a tough one that gives us more action than I think the horse is ready for . . .

3/

4/ . . . I'll simply pull
up and go cut another.

For this horse, we've moved the herd to the side of the round pen—the next step in training. I've cut out a cow and I want to try to drive that cow to the far end of the pen.

The next thing I'll do with him is take the herd to the round pen and settle the cattle on one side of the pen, maybe next to the gate, where they're comfortable standing. Another rider will be in the pen with me, but I never like to work with many people in there, because I don't want a lot of pressure. I can now cut out a cow and work her under very similar conditions that the horse will experience at his first cutting contest. The cattle will be behind us, we'll be moving left and right, but the round pen makes it easier for the horse to control a cow on the sides without getting boxed in a corner.

Training is based on repetition: warm him up, work 20 minutes or so, ride him outside between days of actual training. What ruins so many horses in training is lack of patience on the part of the trainer. The trainer either gets in a hurry with the colt, or there are too many people in there acting as turnback men pressing the cow on the horse, and the result is more pressure than the colt can stand. The result is what I call "cookin' one in the squat."

Let me tell you about cookin' one in the squat. When I was a kid, I used to walk down the road to catch a school bus in front of an elderly couple's house. Each morning, the lady of the house would get up and bake a fresh batch of biscuits—big, beautiful, fluffy biscuits— and I'd always get there in time to have some of those biscuits with them.

But one morning, I looked at that fresh batch of biscuits, and instead of being two inches high, they were only about a half-inch tall. And I asked, "What in the world happened to those biscuits?"

She said, "Well, I tell you, Leon, those biscuits squatted to rise, but I just cooked 'em right in the squat."

I don't make biscuits, but I sure don't want to cook a horse in the squat with too much pressure too soon. It's better to let a horse rise to his full potential before he feels the heat. Never let him know that cutting can be hard for him.

93

1/ As we work, you'll see that I begin to "square up" the round pen. Instead of going around the pen with the cow, we'll work on traveling more back and forth. We'll be far from the herd at times, and we'll be close to the herd. This is where the horse learns to relate completely to the cow, to work at any distance from the herd.

2/

Getting Better

After the horse is working comfortably in the round pen with a herd of cattle on one side, we'll go to the arena with the herd. And this time I'll put the herd on one end of the arena, and spend time driving cattle out of there and working a cow. I'm really going to keep the pressure off of him now. I'll have my help sitting way down at the other end,

or maybe just acting as herd holders to keep the cattle from stringing up the fence. And what I want to do is hopefully drive a cow out of there and take her completely down the arena, working easy, taking a lot of time getting her there. She'll turn around and want to get back, and we'll work her. The horse won't be over-ridden; we'll just work on controlling the cow, breaking clean with her, running and stopping with her,

94

teaching the horse how to handle more pressure through confidence in himself. He'll have to run harder, stop harder, and cope with more of a challenge from that cow. If the horse is progressing the way I want him to, he should be holding a cow on his own, with little assistance from me.

With all that room behind us, back to the herd, I can use inside leg pressure to press the horse off the cow on a hard

run. I can fade back, cut the angle to the side to better control a cow if she starts really pressuring the horse, trying to get back to the herd. Driving a cow this far from the herd gives me room and time to teach him how to control a cow under pressure. There will be some cows, however, that won't allow themselves to be driven that distance. They'll turn around right on the edge of the herd and try the horse, and that's good experience, too.

5/

6/

The horse will get used to working in close proximity to the herd. At this point, the horse is learning a pattern of work, things he'll have to cope with during competition.

What I'm trying to continually teach him in all of this is that he can be ridden away from a cow, to take the pressure off, or if he's back next to that herd, and he has to hold a cow, I can keep him pressed up to the cow with outside leg pressure, and he can get on across the arena and hold. He doesn't have to just keep fading back toward the herd. He holds when I ask him to hold; he gets off a cow when I ask him to. Releasing pressure by getting off a cow not only lets the horse take a slight short cut to the side, in order to turn the cow, it also takes some pressure off the cow, and she won't turn as quickly in a situation like that. Therefore, the horse has even less

pressure to contend with, and more time to control her.

Always keep the horse short on those runs. Keep him just a little short, so when that cow stops, the horse stops, and they synchronize when they turn around and cross the arena.

Problem Solving

Problems we may encounter at this point include the horse wanting to run and head cattle, setting up his own play. In a stop and turn, he may want to take a step toward the cow, or roll out of the turn. The solution is to concentrate on his stops. Use a gentle cow for slow work, a cow that will give you time to stop, back a few steps, then synchronize with the cow through that turn. Use plenty of cow-side leg pressure while stopping, if necessary, to keep him stop-

9/

10/

ping straight, then release that leg pressure after backing so the horse can turn. Throughout this latter stage of training, he will be working mostly on his own, but partly with my hand or hands up, reining him when he needs it, either with one hand on the reins, or for slower work, two hands. If I get into any major problems, either in working around the herd or working the pattern with him, I can always drop back a step. I can work him with the herd in the middle of the

arena, I can work a cow on the fence, so it's one-on-one again; I'll still vary the work between the round pen and the square arena, but the majority of work will be out of the herd in the round pen.

I want to instill in this horse the ability to watch for when a cow stops, and to be prepared for the stop; to be bold enough to step up there and control the cow when I ask him to. I should be able to ride him to a point where he has the advantage over the cow to control and out-

think her. When the pressure is on him, he should let me press him off a cow with my leg to give him more time. I want him to come out of that herd with a lot of caution—to be comfortable but cautious.

By working different cows at various distances from the herd, he'll become comfortable at working wherever I put him in a contest. I'll be able to bring a cow out and begin work wherever I think he will have the best advantage on wild cattle, or wherever I feel he will get the most play out of gentle cattle. On gentle cattle I'll ride him to the cow's advantage, and he will control the situation as it develops. By keeping him short on cattle, I will be able to over-ride him in competition, really ride strong, step him out and head a cow, and when I do he knows he should be on the inside of that cow, so even though we've really headed a cow and made her turn, when he turns he'll try extra hard to get into the ground and get his position to maintain control of the cow after she has turned. This generates more action under slow conditions.

By the sixth month of training, I will also be able to evaluate what kind of style this horse is developing, his strong points and any weak points. I like a horse that can pick up his front end and get through a turn without having to touch down. If he is just sort of walking through the turn, or has to touch down once before he completes the turn, that's when I'll try to get him to clean up that move. That's when I might have to concentrate on more slow work, backing him up a couple steps, waiting a couple seconds for that cow to start moving back across the arena in the opposite direction, then turning him. If he doesn't get plumb over his hocks and make a smooth turn without touching his front feet down on the ground at this point, I'll reach up with a spur and prod him just enough to make him try harder. I'll go back to a snaffle for this type of work, and make sure the horse maintains that eye contact. One cow will be close to us, another may be wandering off quite a distance in the arena, not trying too hard to get back to the herd, but I still want to maintain that eye contact. In competition, when a soft cow is away from the herd like that, you can go ahead and

2/ Backing.

3/ Helping the horse through the turn.

show some work on her by over-riding the horse—breaking left and right with leg pressure, keeping the moves cow-related. The horse will still be concentrating on that cow, even if the cow is a ways off, and that looks good to judges. It also keeps up the horse's intensity.

A horse like that will run, stop, look, and wait if necessary. The only way to develop this is by spending a lot of time waiting and looking. If the rider doesn't

have any "wait" in him, the horse won't, so this turns into a self-discipline thing for the rider, too.

It takes a lot of self-discipline in many ways to train a horse. If the horse is having a bad day, don't get mad and abuse him. That will only confuse the horse and create other problems. Give him the consideration that maybe he is just having a bad day. A lot of times when a horse isn't working up to his potential,

4/ And getting in "sync" with the cow once again.

5/ Good position. Notice how this horse has now "throttled down," so he doesn't get long on the cow.

you'll find the rider isn't riding up to his own potential.

By the time I've had a horse in training eight or nine months, we'll start riding outside with a grazing bit, something light. And I'll work him in this bit periodically. But when I work him with a grazing bit, rather than an Argentine, I will really be aware of what I have on him, so I don't take hold of him too hard and he starts fighting his head or worry-

ing about the bit. Remember, when you lose head control, you lose control of the horse.

After a year of training, if the horse is a good one, he is ready to cut any kind of cattle. I haven't demanded that he become a star, I've asked him to become a star. I haven't demanded that he work to perfection, but I've tried to help him learn to work up to the best of his ability. Training a horse is not unlike raising

1/ Now we're working closer to the herd. I won't work this close too much in the younger stages, however. After a horse has been in training for about a year, I'll work close to the herd and far away, and at all distances in between, right up to Futurity time.

2/

a child. You've got to be strong enough with them both so they respect you, but they'll do a lot more for you out of trust and love, rather than through fear.

A horse may work for a while through fear, but as soon as something happens to break his concentration, he'll probably run off; he may make three good stops, and skip out of there on the fourth one. But if you've built this relationship out of confidence and trust, and he gets in a quakey spot with a hard-to-hold cow, and you help him through it, he'll soon learn to throw his heart over the bar for you.

There are plenty of gimmicks on the market, and some of them may work on some horses if they're in the right hands. If you just can't get a horse to stop, for example, maybe you want to put something on him that will stop him. But the one mistake that many people make when they try a gimmick is this: They're mad at the horse when they try the gimmick, which is usually some type of headgear that can be severe, and when they put it on the horse, they'll really put the crunch on him. Instead of being lighter with something, they'll be stronger with it. The horse might go right through the device, and if that happens there's no place else to go with him.

3/ The calf stops, so we stop and wait and look.

4/ Remember: The horse won't learn to be patient if the rider himself isn't patient.

5/ The calf moves, and the horse moves.

He is hurt and confused, but he has also refused and won. The rider has failed him, and there is no understanding, no harmony, no success.

Showing a measure of compassion and understanding for a horse is part of being a good horseman. I'll admit, it rankles me to see someone at a show who spends a lot of time caring for his horse before the competition, and afterwards, if the horse didn't do good, the horse gets put up in a stall without even being brushed. He's the same horse he was before, and maybe things just didn't work that day, for whatever reason. Number one rule: Take care of the horse, and he'll take care of you.

The Reward

Win or lose, there has to be a reward here. Regardless of how much or how little a person wins, the real reward to the rider or trainer comes from the bond he forms with the horse. Throughout his training, you're developing this horse, teaching him to be smart, building his confidence and style. If he's having trouble understanding something, meet him at least halfway. The trainer is the one who has to offer understanding. In most cases, the horse will do all he can to please, as long as he understands what is expected. Some of the stallions can be bullheaded at times, but I'm talking about horses in general. If he's a good enough horse to go all the way with you, to warrant that much training, and he's believed to be good enough to show somewhere, then he should be given the chance to be the best he can be.

Training horses is fun for me. It's like any other job, in that there is a certain amount of daily stress; and the struggles

1/ Here's another calf that turned back on the edge of the herd. What I'm doing is building confidence in a horse that's being pressed back on the herd. I want to teach him to stay up with that calf, to hold him and work along the edge.

2/ The horse is doing the minimum amount of work to control this calf, which is the proper thing to do. The horse is handling his job, not trying to escape it.

3/ The action gradually picks up, and so does the pressure. To teach the horse to hold next to the herd like this, it's often necessary to use outside leg pressure (leg next to the herd) to keep him pressed up with that cow. As the work continued in this sequence, I also picked up the reins, to help hold him in there.

4/

5/

6/

7/

8/

that are part of life sometimes get in my way. But riding good young horses, being able to feel them make some accomplishment on a day-to-day basis, is still very satisfying to me. If a horse has a problem with being very timid or fractious, I know I can't be rough with him and make it work. I've got to just keep working with him and show him that what I'm asking him to do won't hurt. That he won't get hurt, period. I believe a horse like this requires a lot of petting, getting your hands on him to let him know you like him.

The Made Horse

Once a horse is made, and he's being shown a lot, the main thing I'll do is let him rest as much as possible. I'll work cattle on him maybe a couple times a week, ride him outside, and just really watch his health. I won't keep drilling on him, once I've got him where I want him.

I remember years ago I was riding a good mare and winning more than I ever expected to win anywhere. But still, she wasn't consistently marking as much on the road as she could have been. So I asked my good friend Shorty Freeman about it. I said, "Shorty, I don't understand. I work this mare at home and she is fantastic, and I know she is capable of marking 75s and 76s like clockwork. She feels so great at home. But I don't get that kind of markings at the shows."

Shorty said, "Well, Leon, it's very simple. When you work that mare at home, you never quit her till she's marking a 76. Instead of just working her until she feels good to you, and then

1/ The horse was going a little fast, got long on the cow (out in front), and didn't stop when the cow stopped.

2/ So, I got him stopped, gave him some head direction, and backed him up.

3/ Then we caught up with the cow again.

4/ I've got both hands on the reins and am prepared to help him again if he needs it.

111

5/ But this time he doesn't need it; he stopped and the reins are slack.

leaving her alone, you're getting your high scores at home and then getting 73½ when you go to town."

When I reversed my thinking on that, and started just riding her, working on my riding and showmanship at home, and just getting her stopped a bit and letting her look at cattle, and keeping her responsive, I started winning like a sonuvagun on her. But before, I was leaving it all at home. She was giving me that extra effort when it didn't count. She was peaking at home instead of at the competitions.

I think I was real fortunate when I started in cutting to be around great horsemen like Shorty Freeman, Matlock Rose, and Buster Welch, people who influenced not only me, but really helped shape the sport. There have been many others, too, like Dr. T.K. Hardy, the veterinarian who taught me a lot of things about being on the road with a horse and caring for him, and also how to keep myself mentally right for the game.

When I first started, I told my wife, Myrna, "Someday I hope I can train like Shorty Freeman, cut a cow like Matlock Rose, and have the overall poise of Buster Welch." That's a big order, and I'm still working on it, still learning.

112

6/ *Now, in this turn, I'm back to one hand on the reins.*

7/ *The horse is maintaining good position on this cow.*

8/ We're moving back to the other side of the pen, where we had trouble stopping at the beginning of this sequence. I've got a little inside leg pressure with my right leg to get the flex in this horse so he can make the turn.

9/ And it works. The horse stayed short on the cow, and made another good stop and turn on his own.

10/ And he counter-
acts the calf in an-
other quick move
back the other way.

This mare, Smokin Spook Rio, belongs to my son, Lance. She's four years old, in a grazing bit, and was simply being worked to "tune up" for a cutting. There's no martingale on her, but if Lance thought he would need to work on a lot of head position, involving a lot of direct reining, then he would put on a snaffle and running martingale.

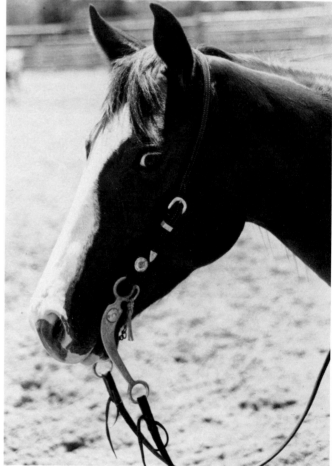

1/ What I want to show in this sequence is the importance of slow work on slow calves, to help keep a horse relaxed and patient.

2/ The horse is working a cow properly; she's not over-reacting, and there's no pressure.

117

3/

4/

5/

6/ Notice how relaxed the mare is. She has a chance to take a breath, and stand there and watch that cow, waiting till it's time to react again. Establishing this ability to wait in a horse is very important.

1/ Cutting in the square arena. Note the horse standing tied in the corner, acting as herd holder. Another horse is positioned in the opposite corner. This is handy when you're short of help; the presence of a horse in each corner helps prevent the cattle from wandering up one side or the other.

2/ Working in the square arena is the final stage in readying a horse for actual competition.

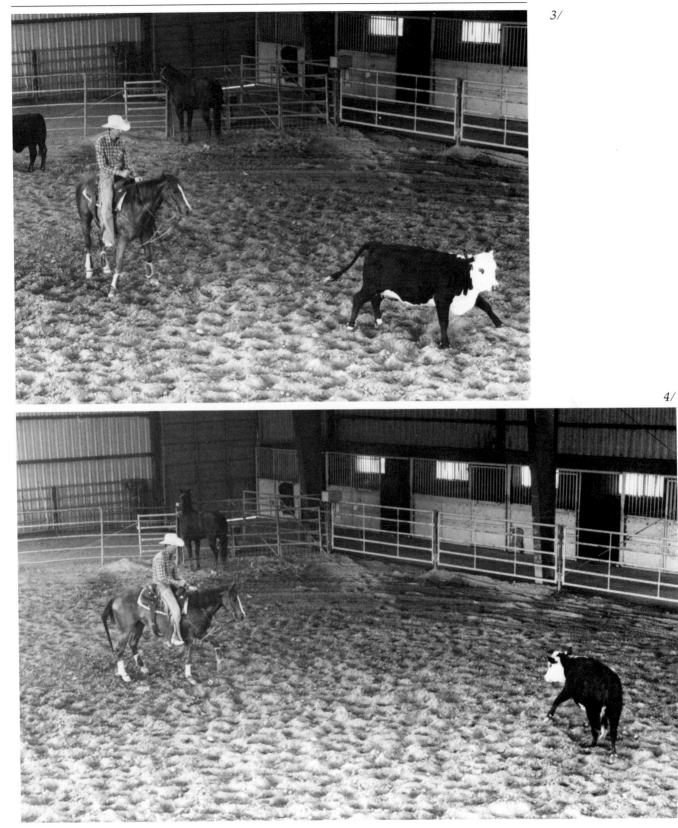

3/

4/

Excellent concentration!

1/ The horse is moving parallel to the cow, working on her own.

2/ We're approaching the side of the arena.

3/ What I want to point out here is the distance from the side fence that I want the horse to stop when a cow goes to the fence. If the cow goes all the way to the fence, I'll probably be off the fence a good ten feet, just to the point where I can still control the cow if she tries to go down the fence to the herd; but I don't want the horse to automatically go clear to the fence. When the calf comes off the fence, that horse can just roll back over the hocks and make a nice flowing move, instead of being pressed against the fence and having to back off of it. When a horse gets to this stage of training, you can always ride him to the fence if you have to, if you think the cow is really going to challenge you on that fence. Too, if a horse is in the habit of automatically turning off the fence, he'll often start using the fence as a crutch, and you won't be able to get the cow off the fence; if the cow even looks to the middle of the arena, the horse is liable to jump in that direction, and his movement will keep the cow trapped on the fence.

123

1/ Even at this advanced stage of training, you'll still have to occasionally correct the horse. In this case, the horse was "ribbing out" toward the cow, so I applied leg pressure to straighten her out.

2/ I also felt she was a little stiff toward the left, and didn't want to flex around in that direction, so I've taken her head and . . .

3/ . . . come all the way around in a pivot with her.

4/ *I made one pivot toward the herd, bending her head . . .*

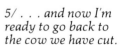

5/ *. . . and now I'm ready to go back to the cow we have cut.*

1/ The sequence now shows this young horse going through some average maneuvers, controlling the cow on her own.

2/

When we advance to the square-type arena, we'll be working under very similar conditions to competition. The horse must be ridden stronger here, to protect the back fence.

4/

5/

6/

7/

9 GREAT HORSES

They're intelligent, athletic, and have been trained through complete trust in their riders.

Smart Date and I won the 1987 Futurity on this calf. Afterwards, I made arrangements to buy the calf and bring her home. I turned her out in pasture and told my help I didn't want to ever see anyone cutting this calf again. The next spring, just for fun, I rode Smart Date out around the heifer.

The great horses that come along in a person's life are few and far between. They're special, and I believe they have to be treated in a special way. The horses I've had that fit into this category have all been intelligent and athletic, and they have all been very sensitive. I suspect that a lot of potentially great horses are ruined in training because of rough hands—people who don't understand this type of horse.

Smart Date is a great mare, and she's very sensitive. This type of horse has

kind of been my specialty through the years; I've done well with them, and that's one of the reasons I asked Shorty Freeman about purchasing her as a two-year-old. I knew she was pretty wild-acting and high-strung. I asked Shorty if he thought this mare would fit me, and he said, "like a glove." And he was right.

The mare is great because everything she does, she does with such enthusiasm. She looks at a cow, a cow looks at her, and I don't feel any softness in her body. Her energy and interest in controlling a cow just come right up through me, and I can feel it. I mean it just gets ahold of me, and the better I ride, the better she performs. If I was to get sloppy on her, it would interfere with her movements, and she wouldn't feel as good.

She can be long-trotting across the arena, and when she stops, she just drops her hindquarters and stops with the same enthusiasm and force that another horse would have in stopping from a lope. She won't try to out-do a cow, she just goes to control her, and as soon as she gets that control, she freezes. The little mare will mesmerize cattle, just like a cat playing with a mouse. There are very few horses like this. There are horses I really like to show, and they have a good feel to them, but there are very few of them that project this intensity on a cow—so much so that it becomes easier for the rider to show well.

Horses like this have been trained through complete trust in their riders. You teach them the job, but they trust you so much in what you ask of them that it never crosses their minds that you might get them into a predicament they can't handle. If they get a little long on a cow, or whatever, you can just ride them through it and they will go back and take control of the job even better than before. Riding through a rough spot means helping the horse—whatever it takes. Taking two hands on the reins and helping the horse get more parallel with the cow, or maybe just pressing the horse away from a cow to take off some of the pressure.

A winning combination: Bob Waltrip, the man who owns Smart Date; the great little mare herself; and trainer/rider Leon Harrel.

Photo by Pat Hall

Correcting mistakes has to be done in a very controlled, subtle manner. If I was to hurt Smart Date, she would really get confused in a hurry. She doesn't want to be punished.

I like everything about this mare. If I'm having a bad day with her, all I have to do is back up, change the circumstances I'm putting her in, i.e., maybe the cattle are too tough on her that day. I'll just take her to the round pen, put her one-on-one with a cow, and just go around with her, and let her relax. Next time I work her with a herd, she won't be trying to get off of cattle; she'll get up there and take care of her job.

131

10 PROFILE: LEON HARREL

As a youngster, Leon aspired to be a world champion cowboy. But he was thinking of rodeo, not cutting.

Leon Harrel grew up on a ranch near Leedey, Okla., which lies between Elk City and Woodward, near the Canadian River. He remembers getting a lot of love and support from his parents, Lance and Doris Harrel. His dad spent plenty of time horseback while checking on cattle and water, or doing other chores he felt were best handled from the back of a horse. From the time Leon was old enough to hang on, he rode behind his dad's saddle, and when he grew bigger

he rode his own horse. Leon liked to help out around the ranch, especially when it involved horses and riding, and much of his spare time was spent horseback as well.

Few children in Oklahoma grow up without being exposed to rodeo; most every town in the state has at least one rodeo a year. Leon harbored thoughts of someday becoming a world champion cowboy. He rode calves, which pitched with him, naturally, and he carried

Leon on Smokey, at the ranch in Oklahoma, 1949.

Leon and Smart Date at the 1987 NCHA Futurity.   **Photo by Pat Hall**

around an old catch rope to practice roping anything that looked like a target.

About the time Leon was ready for high school, he and his parents and two younger sisters, Donna and Darla, moved to Dos Palos, California. An uncle, Woodrow Melton, lived in the area, and he was a team roper. By the time Leon was 15, he and Woodrow were roping together at rodeos, and Leon also started competing in bareback, saddle bronc, and bull riding. At the same time, throughout his high school days, he took in colts to train for others.

Leon's rodeo career was side-tracked after a bull threw him and stepped on his right arm—his riding arm—shattering the bone. He continued to ride broncs and bulls for a while with his left hand, but during that transitional period he

also graduated from high school and went to work for the Triangle T Ranch, owned by G.D. Turnbow, at Chowchilla, California. The ranch was primarily interested in raising Quarter Horses for racing, and Leon broke hundreds of colts, pre-training them for the track. He worked with Sonny Fields, an excellent horseman who was in charge of the horse division.

The ranch's training program assured a home for every horse. Those that looked like they wouldn't make it in racing went into cutting horse training; those that didn't make it in cutting still wound up as well-broke horses, and there is always a market for that kind. Sonny and Leon would gallop race horses in the mornings, and then work with the cutting horses in the afternoons. "At that point in my life, I thought cutting was about the slowest-moving thing

133

I'd ever seen," Leon recalled. "That is, until Sonny gave me the opportunity to start training a cutting horse myself, under his supervision."

The horse was a mare named Barred Georgia, and it wasn't long before Leon started winning on her at some of the area cutting contests. "I began to feel a certain magic on cutting horses, a harmony with them. I gradually became obsessed with cutting," he said.

He was at a horse show in Santa Barbara when he renewed acquaintance with a girl from high school, Myrna Willis. Myrna had grown up on a ranch and loved horses, so she and Leon had a common interest. They were married that same year, 1966, and Leon says it was the best thing that ever happened to him.

"Leon wanted to continue working with horses," Myrna remembered, "and at that time his family was really against the idea. But I was 20 and he was 23; we were both young enough and foolish enough, to decide if horse training was what he wanted to do, then he should do it. He went to work for Mr. Turnbow for seven years, and it was a good foundation for us. The lessons we learned there helped a lot in later years."

Leon turned into a very proficient horse trainer, good enough that the ranch wanted to transfer him to the race-track permanently. He and Myrna had three daughters by then—Hollie, Lesa, and LaDonna—and son Lance was on the way. Leon spent a week at the track and decided that lifestyle wasn't for him. He left the Triangle T employment to strike out on his own, training a variety of horses, including cutting horses, and Myrna was behind him all the way.

They moved to Wild Horse Valley

near Napa, Calif., and Leon purchased a mare named Fizzabar for the Starlight Ranch of Healdsburg, California. "She was a great mare that Don Dodge had ridden and won a lot on," he said. "And I had the opportunity to show her for the Starlight. People said I was crazy to get on a mare like that behind Don Dodge, because there was only one way to go, and that was down. But the mare thought quite a bit of me, and I thought the world of her, and it wasn't long before we were beatin' 'em." He and the mare finished in the top ten that year, 1970, then went to the National Cutting Horse Finals, where they won two go-rounds and the finals, and finished second in the average. Fizzabar was named world champion mare that year by the NCHA.

In 1971, Leon took another horse owned by Starlight, Doc's Date Bar, to the NCHA Futurity. There were nay-sayers in California who warned him that he couldn't go to Texas and beat anybody in Texas. Don Dodge had been the only cutter from California who had ventured eastward and met with real success at the time. But Leon went anyway, and split fourth and fifth at the Futurity with Matlock Rose. "That's when I knew I could compete with them," he said.

The Harrels left Wild Horse Valley and rented a trailer house at Oakdale from their friends, Ed and Modine Smith. By then, Leon had decided he wanted to make a living by solely training cutting horses. "People told me it would be impossible; that there wasn't enough interest in cutting on the coast, and not enough possibilities," he said. "But Myrna had a lot of faith in me, and supported me in my decision, so we

One year at the Oakdale parade. Lance is on Paint, LaDonna is riding Patch, Lesa is on Doc's Nina, and Hollie is mounted on Barred Mac Deck.

Leon with Hollie, LaDonna, and Lance.

made the break from race horses entirely, and have been training cutting horses ever since." Leon trained horses at the Smith place for about a year, and came up with two more NCHA Futurity horses, including Cal's Cindy Ann, a horse he split second and third on for Ed.

That year, he and Myrna purchased their own training facility at Oakdale. "I'll never forget," said Myrna. "It cost us $35,000 for 2.8 acres. We had been staying in the Smith's trailer house at their place, training for them and for others. Ed let us sell the trailer and pay him the difference, so we could raise the down payment on our own place. By the time we got moved, we had spent every dime we had. We had 20-some horses in training, and had to borrow a load of hay from Leon's dad to feed them that first month. But we got through it and then

A ride along the beach in 1974 at Rancho San Augusta.

everything just kind of fell into place."

They stayed in Oakdale for five years, and Leon trained a lot of nice futurity horses; he was in the finals regularly, and had three more horses that finished in the top ten. He won the 1974 NCHA Futurity on Doc's Yuba Lea, owned by PRMCO Ranch.

Myrna smiles when she recalls the annual Oakdale rodeo parade. Leon and all four kids would enter the "family horse division" in the parade, and they would be riding own daughters of Doc Bar. "Folks thought those horses would be crazy at a parade, because they were pretty high-strung," she said. "But they loved it. Doc's Ginger Bar was in there, and Doc's Yuba Lea, and Doc's Tooley Loo, and so forth. Leon would ride in front of the kids, and I'd run along the side of the parade, so if something did happen I could grab hold of a horse. But I never had to."

In 1977, the Harrels sold the stable at Oakdale and purchased an 800-acre farm on the west side of the San Joaquin

Valley. They stayed there until 1983, when they moved to their present ranch at Kerrville. "We made the move to Texas because so many of the NCHA age events are here," Leon said. "It seemed like every 45 days we either had a rig on the road in Texas or were flying to this part of the country, and it just made sense to move here."

The move was memorable for a couple of reasons. Myrna was called away to Santa Barbara at the last minute to be with her mother, who was undergoing surgery, and Leon was left in charge of the caravan. This consisted of a Bronco with a Courier pickup in tow, the family car, a van, three other pickups, and an in-line trailer.

Plus about a dozen people, counting friends who offered to help. Plus five dogs, a cat, and an array of plants, all locked up together in the trailer; and a freezer filled with meat that needed to be plugged in each night.

"We had gear strung around and on top of every vehicle," laughs Leon. "It looked like Ma and Pa Kettle leaving the farm."

The trip took 2½ days of steady driving, stopping at motels for a few hours of sleep each night, and to plug in the freezer. The dogs finally went berserk in the trailer—a Rottweiler broke a window during an escape attempt, and each plant was chewed to pieces.

But, they made it.

"I've had a wonderful life. Four great kids. And Myrna has stood by me through it all. The whole family has been behind me, actually. I remember her dad (Herman Willis, who passed away in 1982) once said Myrna and I were the willing team—she was willing to work, and I was willing to let her. I enjoyed him very much."

"Daddy loved the horses, too," Myrna added. "He was proud of Leon, and really liked to go to the cuttings and visit with all the folks who were there." Myrna's mother, Mildred, lives at Dos Palos; Leon's parents live at Bass Lake, Calif., in the Sierras.

Hollie, Lesa, LaDonna, and Lance grew up horseback, just as their parents did. Hollie was a state champion cutter in California high school rodeo competition; Lesa never showed horses, but turned into an excellent rider; LaDonna competed as a youth in NCHA cutting; and Lance is still cutting. He started winning when he was seven years old, and garnered $12,000 as a non-pro when he was 15. He also tied for 15th in the non-pro division at the '87 Futurity. In 1988 he was in the finals at the Tropicana, in Nevada, and won at other top NCHA contests, including those at Memphis and Augusta, plus the Gold and Silver in Oklahoma and the Super Stakes in Fort Worth. His main interest these days, however, is bull riding, and he has already proven successful in that sport.

Through the years, Leon never really lost his early desire to become a world champion, either in rodeo or some other cowboy sport, but the desire had taken a back seat to his training operation. Campaigning a horse in the open division, all the way to the championship, is an experience akin to rodeoing. It involves a lot of hauling, a lot of time away from home, and of course a lot of winning. The title goes to the horse and cutter who have won the most at the end of the

Behind the Harrel's swimming pool, at the ranch outside of Kerrville, one can look down upon the training stable (below).

year. Leon won the world in 1978, but he didn't set out to win it that year.

"In the '70s, I thought it was important for my career as a trainer to have a horse in the top ten about every other year, and that's pretty much what we did," he said. "But Doc's Playmate was something special. She was a kind mare—not the type that craves a lot of petting, but kind and willing. And she just got better as the year went on. Every time I rode her, regardless of what type of cow I'd cut, or what the conditions were, she would give me 110 percent. And she was only six years old; she had limited showing."

137

Riding Nu Bar.

**Photo by
John H. Williamson Sr.**

Lance's main interest these days is bull riding, and he has already proven to be successful in this event.

On Doc's Playmate.

Photo by John H. Williamson Sr.

They started the year at the Sun Circuit in Arizona—"mainly because it was so rainy in California. We were all tired of the mud and fog, so we all went to the Sun Circuit."

Leon and his mare wound up winning nearly $5,000 at that circuit. "We just grinned and came home," he said. "We felt we had done a good job." They didn't go to any stock shows that winter, or any of the big cuttings.

"There were two other horses that had a big lead on us in winnings, anyway. It was something like $15,000 or $20,000."

The family hauled the mare to some more Arizona shows early in the spring, and then went to several shows in Albu-

querque, and did well again. Then they made a circle around Madisonville, Tex., and won several thousand dollars more. Leon and his mare were sitting about fourth in the standings.

"We still thought, 'Well, maybe we'll end up in the top ten.' We still hadn't considered hauling really hard."

The summer circuit arrived in California, and the pair moved up in the standings. They went to Denton, Tex., for another big circuit of shows, and continued to win. By then, Leon was feeling pretty confident.

"I got to thinking, if I loaded up and went hard for the rest of the year, I might possibly reach that goal I had in

At work in his office at the stable.

On the phone at the edge of the large round pen.

the back of my mind. Myrna and I decided after the Denton circuit that maybe this was the year to go. We decided to take a run at it. From there we just loaded up and went to the shows in Kansas, shows back east at the fairs, down into Louisiana. We were all together, the family and Doc's Playmate, and everywhere we went, we would win. She was good enough and game enough that they couldn't keep us from placing."

From the time they left Denton, it was only about 45 days later that the pair had moved into first place. *The Chatter* is naturally a little behind in results and standings, so the money didn't immediately show up, but Leon knew he was in the lead.

Still, there was some rough hauling involved. Myrna and the girls went home, while Leon and Lance stayed on the road with the mare. Later on, a hired man would take over the rig and care for the mare after a show, and Leon would catch a plane for home, to work on the farm for several days. Then he would fly back to wherever his rig was and switch places with his helper.

"It got a little wild. I remember one time when I was feeling pretty low. I had flown from California to Denver, and picked up my rig and horse; my helper flew back home to work. I got in the truck and drove all night to some shows they had in Kansas. Got there the next

The crew (and mascots) at Leon Harrel Training Stables, Inc., include Dale Parker, Leon and Myrna, Albert Templeton, Lance, Ismael Cano, Guy Smith, and Doug Davis.

morning and showed, then loaded up and left on Saturday night and drove all the way to Fort Sumner, New Mexico. The show was supposed to start at 1 p.m., but there was a delay and it wasn't going to get under way till around 7 that evening. I was tired, and had some time to kill, and some time to think."

He saddled the mare and rode out in a pasture, found his way down to a creek and dismounted. He remembers the day was slightly windy, and he thought about his family. He knew the kids would be starting school the next day.

"I was sitting there, holding the reins, just looking at my mare, and I thought, 'What in the world am I doing here? I'm 1,700 miles from home on a Sunday afternoon at a $250-added cutting in the middle of nowhere.' And I really thought I'd lost my mind."

He showed his mare, won the cutting, and went to a phone to call home.

"I'm coming home," he told them. "My mind is made up—I'm through hauling this year."

Myrna and the youngsters crowded around the telephone. "Aw, Dad," they said. "Don't quit!"

He didn't quit.

"That was the kind of support I had from all of them. It was hard to keep traveling, though we hadn't gone hard like that all year. But I won the championship because I had support from all of them, the family and the mare."

Leon showed Doc's Playmate 65 times that year, and was in the money all but 10 or 11 times.

"The better I took care of her, the better she performed. I didn't have to tune her up; I'd just work her at the cuttings. I'd get her bathed regularly and just made sure she was healthy. A lot of times I'd look for something besides a stall to keep her in. I'd try to find a little place outside of town that had some pasture. To this day, that mare is sound. No blemishes. I had a good horse that wanted to win."

Doc's Playmate was inducted into the NCHA Hall of Fame in 1979, and today she belongs to the San Jose Cattle Company.

When Leon reflects back on his championship year, he doesn't think about "the pats on the back and kind words" that go with winning a title.

"I think about how we all worked together to reach a goal."

—*Randy Witte*

11 TERMINOLOGY

As heard around the cutting horse arena.

Back Fence: Refers to a designated area on the fence behind the cattle. A cutter is penalized three points each time the cow reaches within one step, or three feet, of that area. See Rule 6.

Cutter's Slump: Refers to the posture the rider should maintain while working a cow. Rider's back is relaxed and bent, not straight or rigid.

Herd Bound: A horse that is reluctant to move, to work a cow, when he is in close proximity to the herd behind him is said to be herd bound.

Herd Holders: The two riders, one on each side of the herd, who help the cutter push cattle out of the herd and shape a cow for work. These two riders also prevent the herd from moving up one side of the fence or the other while the cutter is working a cow. It's also their job to prevent any cattle from leaving the herd and interfering with the cutter.

Hiring Help: Just an expression—the help is free. Refers to making arrangements for two herd holders and two turnback riders to help with your run.

Press Off: Use leg pressure—the leg next to the cow being worked—to move the horse away from a cow while working her.

Press Up: Use leg pressure—the leg next to the herd—to move the horse closer to a cow while working her.

Ride Your Horse!: Be more aggressive at riding. Use leg pressure to either press off or press up.

Run: Make your run—it's your turn to compete.

Set for the Stop: Push on the horn and slump down in the saddle, so the horse can really stop; so you don't bounce in the stirrups or move forward. Use slight pressure in the stirrups and keep your heels down.

Shaping a Cow: Getting behind a cow and moving her to a spot in the middle of the arena where you have the advantage to start working her—not too far to the right or left.

Stay Up: Stay up with the cow. Keep your horse parallel to the cow while working her.

Time Line: A mark on the side of the arena, near the herd. When a cutter walks to the herd to make his first cut, time begins when the horse reaches the time line.

A look down one of the rows of stalls at the Leon Harrel Training Stables.

Turnback Riders: The two riders who are positioned farther down the arena, behind the cow that is being worked, and serve as a barrier to keep her from running away from the cutter.

Working Advantage: Staying parallel to the cow being worked, with the horse's head adjacent to the cow's shoulder. Maintaining this position will allow the horse to stop with a cow, but not be so far behind during a turn as to allow the cow to slip behind the horse and return to the herd.

For information on membership in the National Cutting Horse Association, write to:
NCHA
4704 Highway 377 South
Fort Worth, TX 76116-8805

For information on buying/training cutting horses, contact:
Leon Harrel Training Stables, Inc.
1120 Spur 100
Kerrville, TX 78028
Phone: 512-896-7790

Western Horseman Magazine

Colorado Springs, Colorado

The Western Horseman Magazine, established in 1936, is the world's leading horse publication. For subscription information, write: Western Horseman Magazine, P.O. Box 7980, Colorado Springs, Colorado 80933-7980.

Distributed to the book trade by
Texas Monthly Press, Inc.
P.O. Box 1569, Austin, TX 78767-1569
Ph. 800-288-3288